WORKSHOP ORGANISATION

PUBLISHER'S NOTE

This is one of a group of books on industrial relations under the General Editorship of A. I. Marsh, Senior Research Fellow in Industrial Relations at St. Edmund Hall, Oxford.

Workshop Organisation

G. D. H. COLE

with an introduction
to the second edition
by A. I. Marsh

*Senior Research Fellow
in Industrial Relations,
St. Edmund Hall, Oxford*

HUTCHINSON EDUCATIONAL

HUTCHINSON EDUCATIONAL LTD
3 Fitzroy Square, London W1

London Melbourne Sydney Auckland
Wellington Johannesburg Cape Town
and agencies throughout the world

*First published at the
Clarendon Press, Oxford 1923
This edition 1973*

*Printed in Great Britain by litho on antique wove paper
by Anchor Press, and bound by Wm. Brendon,
both of Tiptree, Essex*

ISBN 0 09 114030 7 (cased)
0 09 114031 5 (paper)

CONTENTS

INTRODUCTION TO THIS EDITION

Workshop Organization is one of the three volumes on labour in industry contributed by G. D. H. Cole to the social and economic history of the First World War sponsored by the Carnegie Endowment for International Peace and published in 1923.[1] For many years it has been out of print and available only in specialist libraries and book collections with links with the inter-war period. In the present edition, which is a facsimile reproduction of the original, it will be on general sale for the first time in more than a quarter of a century.

In the field of industrial relations very few works would justify reprinting after so long a period of time. With notable exceptions (including, of course, the vast and seminal studies of Sidney and Beatrice Webb), few have attained high standards of scholarship or had lasting effect upon thinking in the subject ; many have been designed to meet the needs of their own generation and are now only of importance as evidence for the historian. One of the exceptions is, in my view, *Workshop Organization*.

Workshop Organization has not conventionally been thought of as one of Cole's more notable works. The 75 or so books (excluding belles-lettres and detective stories) which he produced between 1913 and his death in 1959 attracted attention for a number of reasons, of which three were outstanding. Some impressed by their intellectual capacity or devotion to their subjects; his first book, *The World of Labour*, and his work on Cobbett might be said to fall in this category. Some dazzled by the force of their polemical brilliance; these included his propaganda publications on Guild Socialism (the principal of which it is also planned to reprint, with modern additions, in this series). A third group, including his *Short History of the*

[1] The two others were *Trade Unionism and Munitions* and *Labour in the British Coal Mining Industry*.

(vii)

British Working Class and (with his brother-in-law Raymond Postgate) *The Common People*, were outstanding for their excellence as student texts and as the contributions of one of the most gifted teachers of his generation.

Commentators have not thought of *Workshop Organization* as falling in any of these categories of notability. It is not a student text in the sense of those cited above; it is certainly not a work of idealistic propaganda. Nor is it readily recognized as an intellectual *tour de force*, though such it undoubtedly is. Had it originally appeared in a more attractive and commercial format it might have been better known, but it would always have stood out as a different kind of work from that usually associated with the name of Douglas Cole.

A simple observation reveals one important element in this difference. Cole was not in the habit of writing to anyone's brief but his own. *Workshop Organization* along with its two companion volumes in the war history were exceptions. He was, as he recounts in Chapter I (p. 1), trying to tell ' as shortly as possible, the war-time history of the shop stewards' movement and kindred industrial developments, and to do so dispassionately, bringing out facts and the opinions which went to the moulding of facts rather than the views of the writer himself '. This was an unusual assignment for Cole, but one appropriate to a sober and semi-official war history, and he was faithful to his charge. Such a study was not calculated to dazzle, however sound its academic achievement might be ; here was no best-seller. Indeed, it has, perhaps deceptively, the appearance of recording clashes of arms and battles long ago.

Perhaps this is why Cole was willing to write so dispassionately about a subject so near to his heart and emotions ; in *Workshop Organization* he has the air, even so soon after the event, of writing about a phase of Trade Union history which to him was over. The Shop Stewards' Movement, as he had known it, was at an end. The ferment of protest against the war, of opposition to the ' stateism ' of the Webbs, of revolutionary socialism associated with the ' stage army of the good ' represented by Cole himself, by Page Arnot, by Mellor and others in the Fabian Research Department, had, by the time of *Workshop Organization*, entered into a new phase. The old, in the rapidly changing context of the times and of youth, could be written up with calm and detachment because, in the spirit in which it first took life, it no longer existed. Other forces had taken over, especially the Communist Party, which Cole deplored.

Cole was in a uniquely good position to record the events of labour history in wartime. As an objector to the war he had, rather oddly as it has seemed to some observers, avoided military service as an adviser to the Amalgamated Society of Engineers (in 1920 the Amalgamated Engineering Union), securing exemption, as someone is said to have remarked with more irony than precision, by doing his best to make the Munitions Acts unworkable.[1] It is surely apocryphal that he was 'responsible' for the new (or not so new) A.E.U. Rule Book, though, as a quick and ready draftsman, he had a good deal to do with it ; but his work evidently left him free to observe as well as to act as Honorary Secretary of the F.R.D. He had a uniquely good position from which to record and flavour the events and tastes of a period the happenings of which might easily have been lost to posterity. For, as he himself confesses, the history of the wartime Shop Stewards' Movement, vigorous as it was, was rarely to be found in documents ; records were scarce ; minutes and notes of meetings and events were quickly dispersed.

It would have been useful if Cole had merely preserved an important piece of social history from oblivion. But he did more than this. The importance of *Workshop Organization*, the factor which principally commends it to

---

[1] Margaret Cole : *Growing up into Revolution*, p. 60. The joke is a good and understandable one, though it has no doubt been overdone. There was, as Mrs. Cole has recalled in a letter to me, much work to be done in advising A.S.E. districts, branches and shop committees about wartime Circulars and Orders and in linking the union to the activities of various government departments in wartime.

INTRODUCTION

attention in 1970, is that the foundations laid by an unofficial, improvised, largely abortive, but widely feared
and spontaneous workers' movement during the First
World War became a springboard for a less unofficial,
more controlled and more secure growth of shop steward
organization in the workshops, first during the Second World
War, and then in peacetime, especially from the middle
1950's. There are two documents without which it is
difficult to understand the current nature and problems
of industrial relations, particularly in the British engineering industry : one is the verbatim report of the Conference
between Federated Engineering Employers and Engineering
Unions during the strike and lock-out of 1897–8 ; the other
is *Workshop Organization*.

This is something which Cole could not have been
expected to foresee in 1922. From the text it is evident
enough that he was reluctant to believe that shop steward
development was at the end of the road after its post-war
collapse. Before his death he was able to chronicle a
revival in shop steward activity, but wrote about it as a
modest development.[1] His anticipations in the middle
1950's were a far cry from the analysis of the Donovan
Royal Commission on *Trade Unions and Employers'
Associations* of 1965–8, and understandably so, since the
evidence available points to the period 1955–65 as a
significant period in the revival of shop stewards, both in
numbers and in workplace bargaining.

The ' two worlds ' of the Donovan Commission Report,
the diagnosis of the ills of British industrial relations as
arising from the myth of national regulation and the all-
too-present reality of workshop bargaining, unstructured and
uncontrolled, have been found by some observers to be
an over-generalized view of the true situation. Undoubtedly
such a criticism is just. Industries have been affected
during the past decade to varying degrees by what Allan
Flanders has dubbed ' the challenge from below '. But the

[1] *Introduction to Trade Unionism*, 1953, p. 55.

(x)

fact remains that, especially outside the public sector, every industry has been affected to a greater or lesser extent by what was once called by George Woodcock, then General Secretary of the T.U.C., the ' pull-down ' of industrial relations to the shop floor. Workshop bargaining has moved in to fill gaps in the systems of different industries. In some the gaps have been greater than in others. And the greatest gaps have been filled in the engineering industry, the same industry in which the Shop Stewards' Movement was born during the industrial turmoil of the First World War.

Workshop Organization has much to tell us from the past about this quieter revolution in industrial relations in which we are still involved. Formal institutions change slowly where Trade Unions and employers are concerned, and attitudes remain disconcertingly frozen in postures inherited from the past. To the general public it often seems that the parties have learned nothing. In its turn, public opinion is stubbornly affected by history. The views on shop stewards of the British citizen and his wife since 1945 have been very largely those translated from the stormy days of 1917 and their aftermath. Their public rehabilitation, if such it can be called, has proceeded at a snail's pace. The fact, as Cole surmised, that ' the somewhat rigid official organization of the Trade Unions presents no obstacle to the rapid growth of fresh forms of organization under an appropriate stimulus from the economic environment' (p. xiii) has perpetuated the impression that stewards are ' wildcats ' as much in revolt against their unions as against their employers. The overwhelming evidence that modern workplace representatives are neither the revolutionaries of the First World War nor the scourges of their own official organizations which was accepted by the Donovan Commission has scarcely yet managed to establish itself in popular belief.

There are further insights in *Workshop Organization* into the attitudes and traditions of craft unions which

INTRODUCTION

remain valuable. The period before the First World War, and that of the war itself, saw a weakening of the determination of craft unions that the despised and suspect phenomenon of ' works unionism ' should be suppressed in the interest of regulation of terms and conditions of work by district committees independent of the workshop and of administration by local branches. It was the watershed between two traditions of job regulation in industrial relations, but one in which the current was never diverted clearly from one channel to another. The problems and dilemmas caused by the persistence of formal craft union structures during periods of intense shop steward activity in the workplace were as evident to Cole as they are to us today, when the lack of identity of the branch with the place of employment and the veto of the district committee may compromise the chances of success of the best-negotiated works and productivity agreements.

Similarly, the attitudes of the same unions to payment by results which developed during the period about which Cole is writing have produced many of the problems and ambiguities with which we are still familiar. From *Workshop Organization* the student can begin to find explanations of the fact that, while ' craft unionism ' in its original sense has withered away under the onslaught of technical change and the willingness of workers to maximize their incomes through management-promoted incentive schemes, the craftsman's attitudes, doubts and fears have remained relatively fixed, yet open to pressure, persuasion and monetary reward. The mixture between conservatism and resistance to change and group and individual pliability in the workplace if the terms are right, the intensely ' political ' nature of the tactics employed by craft union members, are by-products of the past which are as real and relevant to present-day practitioners and students of industrial relations as they ever were.

Most of all, *Workshop Organization* gives an excellent

account of the reasons why engineering employers, between 1917 and 1919, extended recognition to workplace unionism in the *Shop Stewards and Works Committee Agreement*. It was this recognition which provided a jumping-off ground for the new generations of stewards of 1939–45 and of the 1950's, and which furnishes some clue to the 'non-doctrinaire' nature of recent shop steward organization compared with the 'movement' which was necessary to establish a basis for negotiation in the workshops between 1914 and 1918. Of course it is true that Trade Union officials were less hamstrung by legislation during the Second World War than during the first, and that civil servants and politicians were more circumspect in their handling of industrial relations. There was also a sense of national unity in the war effort between 1939 and 1945 which had not existed when the first war broke out. But the fact remains that in 1939, a constitutional basis for the development of workshop relations existed in engineering, the heart of the war effort. What would have happened had it not existed lies in the realms of speculation.

What Cole would have thought about recent developments in workshop relations is perhaps not equally speculative. Their growth by 1959 was notable, but not startling, and more was yet to come. From my own brief acquaintance with him through Trade Union education in the 1950's I think he would have regarded the current scene with some disappointment. Undoubtedly he would have welcomed, as he always did, any decentralization of power as a matter of principle. But it would have concerned him for what purposes that power was being used.

Cole's true sympathy, I believe, would have been not with those pundits who emphasize the beneficial consequences for productivity of an increase in workplace bargaining, or those who fear its possibly inflationary effects, but with those who emphasize its relevance to industrial democracy. And here he would have been dissatisfied with the doctrine that collective bargaining promotes its own form of workers' participation. He ends *Workshop Organization* with a look into the future. The experience of the war could not, he thought, be considered wasted. A mark had been left on Trade Union structure ; the ball had been placed at the feet of workshop leaders to demonstrate their capacity for power in the realization of workers' control, not through the exercise of negotiation itself, but through adoption of the forms of Guild Socialism. It is significant that his terminal paragraphs are concerned, not with the bargaining achievements of the Shop Stewards' Movement, but with the ' collective contract ' and its significance.

It requires very little knowledge of industrial relations to conclude that, since the war, there has been very little movement in this direction, or that there has been a recent revival of Trade Union interest in the doctrine of workers' control. Cole, for one, would certainly have not been satisfied with shop stewards, however militant in collective bargaining, who failed to share his enthusiasms for a socialist commonwealth based upon the workshop. How many shop stewards today can say that they share his belief? Who can say what the consequences will be if they come to do so?

A. I. MARSH
St. Edmund Hall, Oxford

FACSIMILE

OF THE

1923 EDITION

WORKSHOP ORGANIZATION

BY

G. D. H. COLE

OXFORD : AT THE CLARENDON PRESS
London, Edinburgh, New York, Toronto, Melbourne, Cape Town, Bombay
HUMPHREY MILFORD
1923

EDITOR'S PREFACE

In the autumn of 1914 when the scientific study of the effects of war upon modern life passed suddenly from theory to history, the Division of Economics and History of the Carnegie Endowment for International Peace proposed to adjust the programme of its researches to the new and altered problems which the War presented. The existing programme, which had been prepared as the result of a conference of economists held at Berne in 1911, and which dealt with the facts then at hand, had just begun to show the quality of its contributions; but for many reasons it could no longer be followed out. A plan was therefore drawn up at the request of the Director of the Division, in which it was proposed by means of an historical survey, to attempt to measure the economic cost of the War and the displacement which it was causing in the processes of civilization. Such an 'Economic and Social History of the World War', it was felt, if undertaken by men of judicial temper and adequate training, might ultimately, by reason of its scientific obligations to truth, furnish data for the forming of sound public opinion, and thus contribute fundamentally toward the aims of an institution dedicated to the cause of international peace.

The need for such an analysis, conceived and executed in the spirit of historical research, was increasingly obvious as the War developed, releasing complex forces of national life not only for the vast process of destruction but also for the stimulation of new capacities for production. This new economic activity, which under normal conditions of peace might have been a gain to society, and the surprising capacity exhibited by the belligerent nations for enduring long and increasing loss—often while presenting the outward semblance of new prosperity—made necessary a reconsideration of the whole field of war economics. A double obligation was therefore placed upon the Division of Economics and History. It was obliged to concentrate its work upon the problem thus presented, and to study it as a whole; in other words, to apply to it the tests and disciplines of history. Just as the War itself was a single event, though penetrating by seemingly unconnected ways to the remotest parts of the world, so the analysis of it must be developed according to a plan at once all embracing and yet adjustable to the practical limits of the available data.

During the actual progress of the War, however, the execution of this plan for a scientific and objective study of war economics proved impossible in any large and authoritative way. Incidental studies and surveys of portions of the field could be made and were made under the direction of the Division, but it was impossible to undertake a general history for obvious reasons. In the first place, an authoritative statement of the resources of belligerents bore directly on the conduct of armies in the field. The result was to remove as far as possible from scrutiny those data of the economic life of the countries at war which would ordinarily, in time of peace, be readily available for investigation. In addition to this difficulty of consulting documents, collaborators competent to deal with them were for the most part called into national service in the belligerent countries and so were unavailable for research. The plan for a war history was therefore postponed until conditions should arise which would make possible not only access to essential documents but also the co-operation of economists, historians, and men of affairs in the nations chiefly concerned, whose joint work would not be misunderstood either in purpose or in content.

Upon the termination of the War the Endowment once more took up the original plan, and it was found with but slight modification to be applicable to the situation. Work was begun in the summer and autumn of 1919. In the first place a final conference of the Advisory Board of Economists of the Division of Economics and History was held in Paris, which limited itself to planning a series of short preliminary surveys of special fields. Since, however, the purely preliminary character of such studies was further emphasized by the fact that they were

directed more especially towards those problems which were then
fronting Europe as questions of urgency, it was considered best
not to treat them as part of the general survey but rather as of
contemporary value in the period of war settlement. It was clear
that not only could no general programme be laid down *a priori*
by this conference as a whole, but that a new and more highly
specialized research organization than that already existing would
be needed to undertake the Economic and Social History of the
War, one based more upon national grounds in the first instance
and less upon purely international co-operation. Until the facts
of national history could be ascertained, it would be impossible
to proceed with comparative analysis ; and the different national
histories were themselves of almost baffling intricacy and variety.
Consequently the former European Committee of Research was
dissolved, and in its place it was decided to erect an Editorial
Board in each of the larger countries and to nominate special
editors in the smaller ones, who should concentrate, for the
present at least, upon their own economic and social war history.

The nomination of these boards by the General Editor was the
first step taken in every country where the work has begun. And
if any justification was needed for the plan of the Endowment,
it at once may be found in the lists of those, distinguished in
scholarship or in public affairs, who have accepted the responsibility of editorship. This responsibility is by no means light,
involving, as it does, the adaptation of the general editorial plan
to the varying demands of national circumstances or methods of
work ; and the measure of success attained is due to the generous
and earnest co-operation of those in charge in each country.

Once the editorial organization was established there could
be little doubt as to the first step which should be taken in each
instance toward the actual preparation of the history. Without
documents there can be no history. The essential records of the
War, local as well as central, have therefore to be preserved and to
be made available for research in so far as is compatible with public
interest. But this archival task is a very great one, belonging of
right to the governments and other owners of historical sources

and not to the historian or economist who proposes to use them.
It is an obligation of ownership; for all such documents are public
trust. The collaborators on this section of the war history, therefore, working within their own field as researchers, could only
survey the situation as they found it and report their findings in
the form of guides or manuals ; and perhaps, by stimulating
a comparison of methods, help to further the adoption of those
found to be most practical. In every country, therefore, this was
the point of departure for actual work ; although special monographs have not been written in every instance.

This first stage of the work upon the war history, dealing with
little more than the externals of archives, seemed for a while to
exhaust the possibilities of research. And had the plan of the
history been limited to research based upon official documents,
little more could have been done, for once documents have been
labelled ' secret ' few government officials can be found with
sufficient courage or initiative to break open the seal. Thus vast
masses of source material essential for the historian were effectively placed beyond his reach, although much of it was quite
harmless from any point of view. While war conditions thus
continued to hamper research, and were likely to do so for many
years to come, some alternative had to be found.

Fortunately such an alternative was at hand in the narrative,
amply supported by documentary evidence, of those who had
played some part in the conduct of affairs during the war, or who,
as close observers in privileged positions, were able to record
from first or at least second-hand knowledge the economic history
of different phases of the great war, and of its effect upon society.
Thus a series of monographs was planned consisting for the most
part of unofficial yet authoritative statements, descriptive or
historical, which may best be described as about half-way between
memoirs and blue-books. These monographs make up the main
body of the work assigned so far. They are not limited to contemporary, war-time studies ; for the economic history of the war
must deal with a longer period than that of the actual fighting.
It must cover the years of ' deflation ' as well, at least sufficiently

to secure some fairer measure of the economic displacement than
is possible in purely contemporary judgements.

With this phase of the work, the editorial problems assumed
a new aspect. The series of monographs had to be planned
primarily with regard to the availability of contributors, rather
than of source material as in the case of most histories ; for the
contributors themselves controlled the sources. This in turn
involved a new attitude towards those two ideals which historians
have sought to emphasize, consistency and objectivity. In order
to bring out the chief contribution of each writer it was impossible
to keep within narrowly logical outlines ; facts would have to be
repeated in different settings and seen from different angles, and
sections included which do not lie within the strict limits of history ;
and absolute objectivity could not be obtained in every part. Under
the stress of controversy or apology, partial views would here and
there find their expression. But these views are in some instances
an intrinsic part of the history itself, contemporary measurements
of facts as significant as the facts with which they deal. Moreover,
the work as a whole is planned to furnish its own corrective;
and where it does not, others will.

In addition to this monographic treatment of source material,
a number of studies by specialists is already in preparation,
dealing with technical or limited subjects, historical or statistical.
These monographs also partake to some extent of the nature of
first-hand material, registering as they do the data of history
close enough to the source to permit verification in ways impossible
later. But they also belong to that constructive process by which
history passes from analysis to synthesis. The process is a long
and difficult one, however, and work upon it has only just begun.
To quote an apt characterization, in the first stages of a history
like this one is only ' picking cotton '. The tangled threads of
events have still to be woven into the pattern of history ; and for
this creative and constructive work different plans and organizations may be needed.

In a work which is the product of so complex and varied
co-operation as this, it is impossible to indicate in any but

a most general way the apportionment of responsibility of editors and authors for the contents of the different monographs. For the plan of the History as a whole and its effective execution the General Editor is responsible; but the arrangement of the detailed programmes of study has been largely the work of the different Editorial Boards and divisional Editors, who have also read the manuscripts prepared under their direction. The acceptance of a monograph in this series, however, does not commit the editors to the opinions or conclusions of the authors. Like other editors, they are asked to vouch for the scientific merit, the appropriateness and usefulness of the volumes admitted to the series; but the authors are naturally free to make their individual contributions in their own way. In like manner the publication of the monographs does not commit the Endowment to agreement with any specific conclusions which may be expressed therein. The responsibility of the Endowment is to History itself—an obligation not to avoid but to secure and preserve variant narratives and points of view, in so far as they are essential for the understanding of the War as a whole.

J. T. S.

PREFACE

THE complaint that adequate sources of information do not exist is not confined to historians of times long past ; it besets also the chronicler of contemporary events. It has beset me in the writing of this chronicle. The war-time workshop movement in Great Britain was not organized from any single centre or under the auspices of any general organization. Like most living movements in their early stages, it was a spontaneous growth, the outcome of circumstances common to many different areas rather than the creation of any mind or group which made itself the master of circumstances. Attempts were indeed made from time to time to co-ordinate the growing movement, and various organizations, such as the Socialist Labour Party, made more or less successful attempts to influence its development. But on the whole, the workshop movement followed its own course, assuming in most districts approximately the same form, but developing local variations according to local difference of conditions and organization.

Of the great mass of the activities of the shop stewards' movement, no proper records were ever kept, and much that was written down at the time has already been lost or dispersed. The secretaries of the various shop stewards' committees were men working at their trades and possessed no offices at which records could be kept. They may have kept more or less adequate minutes of their proceedings ; but it would be impossible to trace most of these minutes now. Even the scanty and ephemeral printed literature of the movement is not easy to come by : having served its immediate purpose in the locality, most of it went into the wastepaper basket or the fire.

There are, then, no files similar to the records of Government or official Trade Union activity to show the development of the workshop movement. In the writing of this study, I have been compelled to rely mainly on two sources of information. The first and the most important has been my actual memory of affairs with which my war-time work for the Amalgamated Society of Engineers throughout brought me into close contact. This was supplemented by a small collection of records and documents which I collected while the events described were actually in progress. The second source, invaluable for all students of the Labour movement, is the much larger collection of records, notes, and press-cuttings accumulated by the Labour Research Department, to which I must make the fullest acknowledgement. From these two sources, supplemented from Trade Union records and other sources, I have been able to put together, not a detailed account of the way in which the workshop movement developed in different parts of the country, but, I think, an adequate general account of its organization, its aims, its methods, and its relation to the Labour movement as a whole and to the war-time problems with which it attempted to deal. I could have made the study much more detailed, and dealt far more at length with the activities of particular committees; but I found that these were so uniform from district to district that, for the most part, a general survey seemed to be adequate. It appeared, however, to be worth while to preserve in the Appendices a few of the more vital documents illustrating the movement for the use of future students and historians; for otherwise these ephemeral documents may easily be lost or forgotten.

I make no claim to have written a definitive history of the war-time workshop movement. The time for a final judgement on the events of the war period is not yet; for in a very real sense, industrially as well as politically, the war is not yet over, and the final effects of the war-time developments in industrial organization cannot yet be measured. I have tried, for this reason, to keep my personal estimates—not out of my work, which I could not do—but well in the background, and to provide rather a basis for the work of future students than a study which will stand the test of time.

The most vital characteristic of the workshop movement was its spontaneity, or, in other words, the immediate response which the organized workers made to the war-time changes in their conditions or environment. It revealed in Labour organization a great and largely unsuspected power of rapid adaptability to changed conditions. This adaptability involved new problems, no doubt. The rising movement came again and again into collision with the official Trade Union organization as well as with the Government, and its structure remained throughout inchoate and undefined. But, however estimates may differ concerning the good or ill effects of the uprising of the ' rank and file ' which created the workshop movement, the fact that it revealed a considerable power of spontaneous and rapid organization among the workers is not affected. This is important for the future. The conditions which called the movement into being ceased with the ending of the war ; but what has been done once can be done again, and it seems clear that a fresh stimulus would create a fresh movement. How far this would repeat the features of the war-time movement would depend, of course, on the nature of the stimulus, and on any changes in official Trade Unionism that might have taken place. The important point is not that the shop stewards' movement will necessarily rise again, but that the somewhat rigid official organization of the Trade Unions presents no obstacle to the rapid growth of fresh forms of organization under an appropriate stimulus from the economic environment.

In the ordinary sense of the word, the war-time workshop

movement had no leaders. There were men, such as Mr. Arthur Macmanus and Mr. W. Gallacher of the Clyde Workers' Committee, Mr. Peet of Manchester, and Mr. J. T. Murphy of Sheffield, who held positions of big influence among the left wing sections of the shop stewards' movement. But at no time did they occupy, or claim, anything like the position of national leaders of a disciplined and co-ordinated movement. Many of the stewards were ' official ', that is, fully recognized by their Trade Unions, and many more professed no allegiance to the ' left wing ' leaders. The movement was organized throughout on a local basis, and the leading men locally shaped their own policy in accordance with local conditions. When strikes broke out and spread from district to district, this was far less in response to any general strike-call from the centre than because the same conditions produced in different areas the same response. Sympathy, of course, accounted for much in the spread of the movement; but the decision of other districts to take part in a strike initiated in one area was made locally, and at least as much on the strength of newspaper reports as of any organized propaganda. No shop stewards' strike movement ever became general, even within the industry in which it originally broke out.

In short, the movement was a rank and file movement, which theoretical influences helped to shape, but did not create. It was a local movement, originated separately in each area as a response to a certain set of conditions. And it was a spontaneous movement, and not one engineered by a few ' agitators ', although the few ' agitators ' doubtless helped to develop it. In these characteristics lies its main interest for students of Labour history, that is, of the response of the working class to changes in its economic environment.

G. D. H. COLE.

February 1922.

CONTENTS

CHAPTER I

INTRODUCTORY

DURING the war the words ' shop steward ' came, in the mouths of many people, to signify a very high degree of wickedness and perversity. It was the shop stewards who were preventing Great Britain from winning the war, who were wantonly stirring up strikes, who were in league with Germany to prevent the prompt delivery of munitions which were urgently required at the front, and who, though they were themselves an insignificant minority of the workers, most of whom were ' sound at heart ', were, so it was thought, somehow successful in leading their innocent fellow-workers by the nose. The following study is an attempt to tell, as shortly as possible, the war-time history of the shop stewards' movement and kindred industrial developments, and to do so dispassionately, bringing out facts and the opinions which went to the moulding of facts rather than the views of the writer himself. I hope that the readers of this study will be able to form from it a clearer idea of the character and achievements of the war-time workshop movement than would be possible on the basis of the incidental references to it in other studies or the—for the most part ill-informed—comments of the Press.

The workshop movement of 1914 to 1918 has none of the neatness and precision which are possible only in organizations made to order, in pursuance of a definite plan executed by a controlling will. It was a spontaneous movement, arising naturally and inevitably out of the industrial circumstances of the time, in many places simultaneously. One district and group did indeed learn from and imitate another ; and there were certain theoretical influences which went to the making of the movement, especially on its unofficial side. But the movement itself was spontaneous wherever any considerable number of workers was assembled for the manufacture of munitions of war, and the influence of one district on another, and of the various schools of Labour theorists on the movement as a whole, was confined to developing it and endeavouring to influence its policy and give to it a more definite form and structure. The circumstances of war-time industry led, naturally and inevitably, to workshop organization ; and organization on a workshop basis would have arisen, although it might have taken to some extent a different direction, if there had been neither a Marxist, nor a Guild Socialist, nor any other sort of industrial theorist, from one end of the country to the other.

The mere fact of working together, within a system which conditions the actions of the whole group, naturally engenders a certain sense of solidarity and some capacity for common action. But circumstances may prevent this solidarity and capacity from finding expression. To a great extent they had been so prevented in Great Britain up to the outbreak of war. Loyalty to a particular Trade Union, which enrolled only some of the workers in many different factories, was more keenly felt, as a rule, than the common solidarity of all the workers, belonging often to as many as a dozen different Unions, working in a particular shop. The circumstances of Trade Union development, and the questions on which Trade Union action had been mainly concentrated, had, as we shall see, tended to encourage this attitude, and to discourage the growth of the workshop spirit. Workshop and Works Committees were largely regarded as anti-Trade Union devices, of which particular employers had made use in order to keep their employees out of the ranks of the Unions. Shop stewards, with very limited functions, were indeed familiar in a number of industries, and not a few Trade Union Works or Shop Committees did exist ; but these were not regarded as possessing any particular significance from the Trade Union point of view.

Yet, within a year of the outbreak of the war, the shop stewards' movement was in full operation in most of the important centres of munitions manufacture, and was rapidly developing and gaining fresh powers and functions. The Trade Unions, in response to the Government's call, had agreed to the temporary surrender of the right to strike, and to the imposition of considerable restrictions on workshop freedom and on free mobility of labour; and the shop stewards, not fully recognized by the Trade Unions and not parties in a direct sense to the concessions which the Unions had agreed to make, found the leadership of militant action in the munitions industries devolving upon them. The war-time movement first took definite shape in connexion with a strike—the Clyde engineers' strike of the early months of 1915; and, from the first, it found itself in open hostility to the Government, and to some extent also to the official Trade Union leaders. The majority of the stewards were, it is true, throughout ' official ', in the sense that they were to some extent ' recognized ' by the Trade Unions to which they belonged; but the Union rules under which they were supposed to work made no provision for such situations as arose in the workshops almost daily under pressure of the peculiar conditions created by the war, and consequently even the ' official ' stewards found themselves constantly impelled to take unofficial action, and greatly to exceed the powers officially conferred upon them.

Yet it would be a great mistake to conclude, from the fact that the shop stewards were actively associated with almost every important strike or dispute in the munitions industries during the war, that the sole or main pre-occupation of the great majority of them was the stirring up of unrest. Unrest, indeed, came a great deal their way, and some of them helped a good deal in giving it form and direction; but the main activities of most of the stewards and other workshop representatives were concerned with the countless difficulties which arose in the readjustment of conditions which had to be made in order to adapt the industries of Great Britain to the needs of war. ' Dilution ' in particular, that is to say, the introduction of less skilled workers to eke out the labour of those already in the industry and to take the place of those who were called away for military service, involved continual re-arrangements and alterations in the organization of the shops and in the methods of production and the established rules of workshop practice. Almost every one of these readjustments was a potential source of friction and dispute; and the fact that the vast majority of them were accomplished without trouble shows that the shop stewards played a big part in preventing and settling difficulties as well as in conducting disputes. It would have been impossible without strong workshop organization among the workers, to carry out the changes which were indispensable; and this has to be borne in mind in any judgement that may be passed on the activities of the shop stewards' movement.

As we shall see in this study, the shop stewards' movement as a whole has, to some extent, to be distinguished from that wing of it which attracted the greatest public opinion. ' Labour ' is usually mentioned in the Press and in conversation in direct proportion to the amount of unrest and industrial dislocation which exist. When there is a big strike, the papers are full of it. When work is proceeding normally, ' Labour ' ceases to figure in the Press.

So it has been with the shop stewards. They are known to the public as the active leaders of the most important war-time strikes in the munitions industries; but almost nothing is known of their more humdrum daily activities. I have tried in this study to preserve the balance, and to tell the story, both of their militancy and of the work which they did, far more unobtrusively, as the workshop representatives of Trade Unionism in dealing with all manner of industrial grievances and problems. In order to avoid burdening the text unduly with long quotations, I have relegated to the appendices many of the documents bearing upon the subject. The reader would be well advised to refer to these as they arise in the course of the discussion in the chapters to which they relate.

CHAPTER II

WORKSHOP ORGANIZATION BEFORE THE WAR

THE idea of workshop organization among Trade Unionists, to which the events of the war years in Great Britain as in other countries gave so great an impetus, is of course by no means new. Many of the earliest Trade Unions began in effect as works clubs or companionships, formal or informal associations of the workers employed by a particular establishment. Even when Trade Unionism became a general movement, many local trade societies and many branches of larger bodies continued to consist of workers drawn either from a single works or factory, or from a group of neighbouring and closely related works. Indeed, it may be said that Trade Unionism in its early stages was based on works organization to a larger extent than it is to-day, and that the growth in the number of industrial establishments and in the strength and universality of the Trade Union movement has been partly responsible for destroying the works basis which it originally possessed. This destruction, in its turn, has been felt as a source of weakness, and has led to a growing demand for the re-creation of organized units, centring round a single establishment, within the larger Trade Union bodies.

As Trade Unionism grew from infancy to adolescence, the scattered trade clubs, of which there were in many cases several in a single town organizing the same classes of workers, showed a tendency to re-group themselves in larger and more formidable bodies. This took place to a large extent when the Builders' Union and the Grand National Consolidated Trades Union were formed during the great Labour upheaval of 1832 to 1834. Thereafter, these large organizations fell asunder; but many of the trade societies out of which they were built up remained in existence, and formed the nuclei for the later development of Trade Unionism on a national basis.

From 1850 onwards the local trade societies which had
survived, or came into existence subsequently to, the collapse
of 1834 were gradually being consolidated into powerful national
Unions, which have maintained a continuous existence up to
the present time. The effect of this consolidation was the
fusion, into larger local branches of the new national Unions, of
many of the local trade clubs which had previously centred
round a single factory, so that all the organized workers belonging to a single craft or group of crafts in a particular town came
to be organized in one branch of a single national Union, or
perhaps in rival branches of two or more overlapping national
Unions. Although in some cases local trade clubs survived,
the works basis of organization generally disappeared in the
majority of industries ; for the new ' amalgamated ' Societies
did not, in most cases, preserve any special organization in the
particular works in which their members were employed.

From this time onward, although there was more than one
setback, the numerical strength of the Trade Unions grew
steadily. Consequently, the membership of the larger ' Amalgamated Societies ', such as the carpenters and the engineers,
in the more important centres grew rapidly, until it was no
longer possible for all the local members to meet as a single
branch. Branches were accordingly divided, and new branches
were opened as occasion arose in towns in which there were
already branches in existence. This division, however, almost
always followed the lines, not of the members' place of employment, but of their residence. Thus, the members living in
South Leeds, wherever they might be working, enrolled themselves in the South Leeds branch of their Trade Union, and the
members living in North Leeds, even if they were working in
South Leeds, joined the North Leeds branch. Thus, not only
did each branch as a rule include workers employed in many
different establishments: the workers employed in a single
establishment and belonging to the same craft were often
organized in several different branches of the same Society.

At the time when this growth of Trade Unionism began to
occur, and indeed almost up to 1914, the new Amalgamated

Societies, apart from their activities as benefit societies, were concentrating mainly on the attempt to secure recognition of certain broad principles, of which the most important was the right of ' collective bargaining '. In other words, they were seeking to establish the principle that, over a whole area, certain standard rates of wages should be paid, and certain recognized hours and conditions of labour respected, and that these wages, hours, and conditions should be determined by negotiation between the Trade Unions and the employers concerned. These questions, although they sometimes led to difficulties as to the precise way of applying them to particular establishments, were for the most part not workshop questions, but matters applying equally to all establishments in a particular industry and area. Accordingly, while Trade Unionism was passing through this phase, the need for distinct workshop organization was usually not apparent, and it was even often contended that ' works unionism ' was the worst enemy of Trade Unionism, since it might become the instrument by means of which the employer would evade the recognition of the uniform conditions established by collective bargaining for all the workers in the trade and in the district concerned. In most occupations, therefore, no regret was felt as the works basis of Trade Union organization was gradually superseded, and most Trade Unionists were not at all conscious of the need for it. The problem of the period was for them the successful establishment of standard or minimum district conditions : the insistence was all on the uniformity of conditions throughout the trade, and not on diverse problems arising in particular establishments.

Naturally, the workers in all industries were not affected equally or in the same way by this subtle process of change in the basis of Trade Union organization. The miners, for example, hardly experienced it at all. They were, it is true, gradually consolidating their isolated ' pit ' lodges or clubs into wider district or county Unions ; but the character of their industry itself caused the branches of these Unions to be based as a rule on a particular pit or group of two or three pits associated with

a single mining village. Pit organization, with mass meetings
at the pit-head for the determination of questions of policy,
thus remained, and has remained up to the present time,
a characteristic feature of Trade Unionism in the mining
industry. With it the growth of County Miners' Associations,
and their subsequent linking-up into a single national body,
the Miners' Federation of Great Britain, has not interfered in
any considerable degree. This fact helps to explain the essentially democratic character of the miners' organizations and
their comparative immunity from some of the problems of
Trade Union government which have been actively disputed in
other industries.

The second case in which Trade Union organization on
a works basis has a long and continuous history is the printing
industry, where the printers' ' chapels ', actually antecedent in
the case of the compositors to any other form of Trade Unionism,
have maintained to the full their strength and importance in
the industry up to the present time. As other trades besides
the compositors in the printing and paper industry have become
organized, they have imitated the ' works chapel ' form of
government, and practically every Union in the industry has,
as its smallest unit of administration, the group of members
employed in a particular shop or works. Moreover, as the
various Unions in the industry have drawn together into an
inclusive federation—the National Printing and Kindred Trades
Federation—provision has increasingly been made for joint
action between the ' chapels ' of the different trades. ' Federated
House Chapels ' have thus come into existence, and, in the
newspaper industry, the journalists, as well as the manual
workers, have formed their chapels and linked up with the
other Unions for common action.

It is difficult to form any accurate estimate of the extent
to which various forms of workshop organization existed in the
Trade Union movement in most other industries before the war ;
for, when it existed, it was often informal, and few references
to it can be found in the official publications of the Trade
Unions. In many cases their rule books did, indeed, make

provision for the appointment, in works, shops, and departments, of delegates of the Trade Unions, to whom certain minor
administrative functions were entrusted. These were called by
many different names—' shop stewards ' or simply ' stewards '
in the engineering industry ; ' delegates ' or ' walking delegates ' in certain trades in the building and shipbuilding
industry ; ' works representatives ' in certain of the minor
metal trades ; and so on. As a rule their functions were, in
theory at least, very limited, and they possessed no discretionary
or negotiating powers to act on behalf of the Unions to which
they were responsible. It was their duty to carry out periodical
' card inspections ' among the Union members in the works, for
the purpose of ascertaining whether the members were entered
on their Trade Union cards as ' fully paid-up '. They had also
to interrogate all fresh workers who were taken on as to their
Trade Union membership, and if they were non-unionists, to
endeavour to enrol them. They were expected to be ready to
receive complaints from any man in their trade working in the
shop, and to keep a regular watch on events in the shop. But
at this point their official functions ceased. If members were
in arrears with their contributions, or if some Trade Union
principle was threatened by any action taken by the management or by a section of the workers, they were expected to
report upon the case to the district officials of their Trade
Union, who would then take the matter up and deal with it
through the recognized forms of negotiation, or by the methods
established inside the Union itself. The shop steward had no
official right to negotiate with the foreman or the management
if a grievance arose inside the shop. He was not officially
recognized by the management ; and the district and national
Trade Union officials could not, constitutionally, delegate to
him any part of their function of collective bargaining. Apart
from the enrolment of members, his function was to keep his
eyes and ears open and to report upon developments. The
district and national Trade Union machinery was supposed to
do the rest.

It is easy to see that this form of ' shop-stewardism ' arose at a time when the attention of the Trade Unions was concentrated, not upon workshop problems, but upon the more general issues of collective bargaining. If the Unions were to make good, in their earlier days of struggle, it was indispensable that they should secure from the employers the recognition of their right to negotiate collectively on behalf of their members. It was natural that, in striving to establish this right, they should, as far as possible, concentrate their energies on the attempt to secure the universal acceptance of one or two very simple, but also from their point of view, very important, principles which could be so stated as to apply equally to the whole of their members. The obvious principles first to be established were those of the guaranteed minimum, or standard, rate, and the recognized normal working week. The Unions set out to secure that, in any district, every member belonging to a particular trade should receive at least a certain fixed and definite occupational rate, and that this rate should be paid for, at most, a certain limited number of hours' work per week. Clearly, these principles were equally applicable to all members of the Union, and, so far as they were concerned, the only questions that could arise in a particular works were whether or not the standards of wages and hours laid down for the district as a whole were being observed. The object of the Unions was to persuade all firms in the district either to observe these standard conditions without written agreement or to enter into a written agreement guaranteeing their observance. In either case, the failure by their employer in a particular works to observe the standard conditions was not a works but a district question, since a failure to enforce the conditions in one works would break the charmed circle and threaten the maintenance of the standard elsewhere. It was therefore for the Union district as a whole, rather than for its representatives in any particular works, to deal with grievances when they arose, and the function of the works representatives was limited to the reporting of any difficulty arising, in order that the District Committee and officials might have the necessary data on which to take action.

This is the historical explanation of the scant importance attached to workshop organization in the official constitutions of the Trade Unions in the great majority of ' factory ' industries before the war.   But the theory was never, fully and everywhere, operative in practice.   Some Trade Unions, indeed, made no provision at all for workshop organization, and the reporting of troubles arising in the shops was left to the spontaneous action of any member or group of members who might have a grievance.   In such cases, as practically throughout the textile industries, members might either report difficulties direct to their district secretary, or might raise them at the next branch meeting of their Union, and so get them officially taken up.   A good many grievances, however, under this system inevitably escaped the notice of the Union, at least until it was too late to prevent them from flaring up into serious trouble.

In other cases, as in the engineering industry, where the rules of most of the Trade Unions made definite provision for the appointment of ' shop stewards ', varying results followed. In some areas the practice of appointing stewards either was not taken up, or fell entirely into desuetude, so that the position was the same as in the textile industries.   In other areas, stewards were appointed under the rules of the Unions, and confined themselves more or less rigidly to doing the work contemplated in the rule books.   Where this was the case, very considerable difficulties were often experienced in keeping the organization up to the scratch; for, especially in highly organized shops, the duties tended to be of a purely routine character, and accordingly it was both difficult to find men willing to undertake them, and still more difficult to prevent slackness from arising in their performance.   In yet other areas, and in a number of particular works, the development took a different line, and the stewards, while performing the work officially prescribed for them by their Unions, also undertook many other duties, and became, in certain instances, a powerful factor in the safeguarding of the workers' interests within the shop.

In the engineering and kindred industries in which the

' shop steward ' system had, even before the war, the strongest hold, the accretion of additional powers in the hands of the stewards was particularly marked in those works in which systems of ' payment by results ' were largely in operation. This must not be taken as implying that ' payment by results ' is always more favourable than time-work to the growth of workshop organization ; for this had not been at all the case in the textile industries, in which ' payment by results ', in the form of piece-work, is almost universal. But, in the engineering and kindred industries, and also to some extent in coal mining and in other industries of various types, the increase of ' payment by results ' in all its forms had undoubtedly given a very powerful stimulus to organization on a works or workshop basis.

The explanation of this difference is simple. The textile industries (and also nearly all branches of the iron and steel industries in Great Britain) are highly standardized, and are almost wholly engaged in the repetitive production, by means of standardized machinery, of standard types of product. This is most clearly true of the cotton industry, where the standardization of plant and process is almost complete, where the rate of production is largely determined by the power-house, and where, although there is a very wide diversity of product, the piece-work price for each product can be calculated, with almost mathematical accuracy, with the aid of the standard price lists agreed upon by collective bargaining between the Trade Unions and Employers' Associations in the industry. There is, as we shall see later, some room for workshop disputes left even in the cotton mills ; but few of those are traceable to the working of the standardized system of ' payment by results '.

In most branches of the British engineering and kindred industries, and particularly in those in which the skilled workers are mainly engaged, the position was before the war, and still to a very great extent remains, essentially different. Piece-work and other forms of payment by results have not been introduced into these industries under national agreements between the big Trade Unions and Employers' Associations, carefully regulating their precise method of operation, and reducing the assessment of a particular piece-work price or ' basis time ' to a purely mathematical calculation. Where they have been introduced, it has been shop by shop, and often job by job, and without any collective Trade Union regulation beyond the insistence that the district standard time-rate of wages shall be paid to every skilled worker engaged under a system of ' payment by results ', irrespective of his output. Moreover, there is not, in the great mass of British engineering operations, any standardization at all approaching that which exists in the textile industries. The work done is still largely of a jobbing character, or, even if process are repeated, for skilled men at least the ' runs ' are, as a rule, comparatively short. Consequently, new piece-work prices and basis times have constantly to be arranged for fresh operations, while the fact that the machinery also is by no means standardized means that the price for the job has not infrequently to be modified in accordance with the character and equipment of the machine-tool on which it is to be done. Bargaining for new prices is therefore almost always proceeding, and practically the whole of this bargaining is carried out separately in each shop, if not for each particular operative.

The introduction of ' payment by results ', in any and all of its forms, has been made, as a rule, in face of more or less definite opposition from the engineering Trade Unions. It was one of the principal issues in the great national engineering lock-out of 1897, and in the agreement by which that dispute was brought to an end the employers secured, on paper at least, the right to introduce ' payment by results ' in any form which they might choose to adopt. The actual clauses bearing on this point in the 1898 agreement are as follows :

> The right to work piece-work at present exercised by many of the Federated Employers shall be extended to all members of the Federation and to all their Union Workmen.
> The prices to be paid for piece-work shall be fixed by mutual arrangement between the Employer and the Workman or Workmen who perform the work.

The Federation will not countenance any piece-work conditions which will not allow a Workman of average efficiency to earn at least the wage at which he is rated.

The Federation shall recommend that all wages and balances shall be paid through the office.

In the revised agreement of 1901, this form of words was replaced by the following more favourable clause :

Employers and their Workmen have the right to work piece-work.

The prices to be paid for piece-work shall be fixed by mutual arrangement between the Employer and the Workman or Workmen who perform the work, and the Employers guarantee that they shall be such as will allow a Workman of average efficiency to earn at least his time-rate of wages, with increased earnings for increased production due to additional exertion on his part.

The Federation will discountenance any arrangement or re-arrangement of prices which will not allow a Workman to obtain increased earnings in respect of increased production due to such additional exertion, and the Trade Unions will discountenance any restriction of output.

The Federation agree to recommend that all wages and balances should be paid through the office.

A mutual arrangement as to piece-work rates between Employer and Workmen in no way interferes with the Trade Unions arranging with their own members the rates and conditions under which they shall work.

Thus, the result of the dispute of 1897 was to give an impetus to the movement for the introduction of piece-work and similar systems, and at the same time to give collective sanction to the method of purely individual bargaining on all questions of piece-work prices. Under the curious name of ' mutuality ', this method became firmly established over a considerable part of the industry, and piece-work prices were frequently arranged, especially for the more skilled types of work, by the foreman and the workman who was to do the job striking a bargain for a single piece of work, and then, when another job came along, striking another bargain, and so on.

It was, however, obvious that matters could not rest at this point. When a particular job recurred often in a particular shop, a standard price for it was naturally evolved. Moreover, it was inevitable that the prices accepted by one man should react upon the prices which other men in the same shop could obtain from the foreman. Consequently, it became, in most well-organized shops, a regular practice for informal consultations to take place between a few of the men before any questionable price was accepted, and for groups of men to take up the question of any objectionable price with the foreman or the management. In some works, these informal consultations served as a basis for a more formal organization ; and special ' Workshop Committees ' or ' Piece-work Committees ' sprang up for the purpose, among others, of considering all prices before any man was allowed to accept them. In Crewe railway workshops, for example, there arose ' Piece-work Committees ', which kept ' books of prices ' for the various trades, and, by the gradual accumulation of precedents, worked out something like a standard price-list for the whole establishment, the list of course being modified, as need arose, for each fresh job or new method of doing an old job.

In this case, as in a good number of others, the ' Workshop Committee ', under one name or another, secured *de facto* recognition from the management, whose representatives met it for the discussion and adjustment of piece-work prices and other workshop difficulties. In a few cases, recognition by the employers was carried considerably further, and the secretary of the Committee was accorded special facilities for negotiation with the rate-fixers employed by the firm, with, in at least one case in Glasgow, an office of his own in the works and full access to all departments for the purpose of dealing with workshop grievances. In other cases the management extended no recognition to the Works Committee, which pursued its work independently. The method of ' mutuality ' in these instances remained theoretically in full force ; but the Works Committee was, in fact, frequently consulted by any worker who was offered a new price, and, in case of need, the Committee could usually succeed in interviewing the management, if not *as* the Committee, at any rate as a ' deputation from the men '.

Where workshop organization of this kind existed, it was

sometimes closely related, and sometimes wholly unrelated, to
the organization of official shop stewards provided for in the
rules of most of the Unions. Sometimes the shop stewards, or,
in large works, the chief stewards, from each shop or department, were the Works Committee, or formed the principal
element upon it. In other cases there was often no shop
stewards' organization at all, or the stewards, if they existed,
stuck to their official ' reporting ' functions, and left workshop
bargaining to the Works Committee as a separate organization.
There was no general rule, for the whole development of workshop bargaining was sporadic and unregulated.

Thus, even where stewards or Works Committees had
achieved a considerable measure of recognition from employers,
their status in their own Unions was often extremely doubtful.
Under the National Executive Council, most Unions in the
manufacturing industries have District Committees, to which
the work of local organization and negotiation, often with a high
degree of local autonomy, is entrusted. The shop stewards are
responsible to the District Committee, by which, in theory at
least, their appointment by the workers in the workshop has
always to be formally ratified. Any extension of the functions
of the shop stewards, and any Trade Union recognition of Works
or Workshop Committees, would therefore require, in the first
instance, to be made by the District Committee, subject to the
general rules of the Trade Union, and to such over-riding powers
as might be vested in the National Executive. Sometimes,
before the war, a particular Trade Union District Committee
had taken some steps towards either a formal extension of the
powers of shop stewards or a formal recognition of Works
Committees ; but more often the position had remained undefined, and the District Committees of the Unions had contented themselves with a *de facto* recognition of the developing
workshop machinery.

The position was complicated by the fact that, even before
the war, both District Committees and National Executives
were to some extent jealous of the growth of the new forms of
workshop organization. The basis of Trade Unionism in most

of the industries concerned was a ' craft ' basis, and there were accordingly, as a rule, a number of different Unions represented among the organized workers in any considerable establishment. During the years 1910–14 a strong movement developed among the workers in almost all industries in favour of the amalgamation of their rival and overlapping ' craft ' Unions into bodies formed on a broader basis, and seeking to organize all workers in any particular industry, ' without distinction of craft or skill, grade or sex '. This movement made considerable headway, and naturally expressed itself partly in the desire for closer co-ordination among all grades of workers in the workshop itself. The inchoate and unregulated tendency towards workshop organization was naturally in intimate connexion with this amalgamation movement, which was for the most part a ' rank and file ' movement of a left-wing character, keenly critical of the attitude and conduct of the permanent Trade Union officials.

Hence, the growth of workshop organization became connected, in the minds of the Union officials, and to a great extent in reality also, with the rise of ' left-wingism ' inside the Trade Union movement. This made the officials far less inclined than they might otherwise have been to put their energies into stimulating workshop organization, and far more reluctant to agree to extended powers or definite recognition of the developing force. The tendency, which would probably have manifested itself in any case, for the workshop movement to develop along unofficial lines, and even sometimes in hostility to official Trade Unionism, was therefore present to some extent even before the circumstances of the war gave to it a marked additional stimulus. This point will be much more fully discussed in a later chapter.

Nevertheless, until the war came, no one apart from those immediately affected, was paying any particular attention to the problem of workshop organization. In all the manifold discussions which took place in Great Britain between 1910 and 1914 concerning the basis of Trade Union organization and policy, the questions of shop stewards and organization on

a works basis were very little discussed. The 'Industrial
Unionists', who drew their inspiration from the American
'Industrial Workers of the World', had, indeed, something to
say about the superior combative efficiency of 'plant unionism'
over 'craft unionism', and the Guild Socialists were beginning
to stress the fundamental importance of works organization for
the winning of workers' self-government in industry. But these
were still voices crying in the wilderness, and among Trade
Unionists generally the question was very little discussed. It
was the *bouleversement* of industrial conditions resulting from
the war that made workshop organization immediately a front-
rank Trade Union problem.

Indeed, all the pre-war developments of the workshop movement were on a very small scale, and were conducted in practical
isolation one from another. Probably the most powerful pre-
war works organization of Trade Unionists, and the most fully
recognized in practice by the Trade Unions to which the
members belonged, was the Royal Arsenal Shop Stewards' Committee at Woolwich. Most of the skilled trades in Woolwich
Arsenal had their stewards, and these had not only secured the
recognition of considerable negotiating powers concerning piece-
work prices and conditions generally from the management, but
had also firmly established their position in relation to their
own Trade Unions, which, on account of the special conditions
of work in this huge Government-owned munitions factory,
largely allowed the works body to do its own negotiating, and
to determine its own policy within the general policy of the
Unions. This, however, was recognized as an exceptional case,
and had little influence on the position elsewhere.

It should be noted that, in most cases, the pre-war workshop organization was confined to skilled workers, who were by
far the most strongly organized, and alone possessed a marked
tradition of solidarity. The less skilled workers were, in most
cases, unrepresented upon, and unconsulted by, the workshop
bodies. Nor were there in many cases inclusive bodies representing even the whole of the skilled men. Often the shop
stewards of a particular trade or group of trades acted in com-

plete isolation from the stewards, if there were any, who represented other trades or groups. Works and Workshop Committees of a Trade Union character were quite exceptional, and no attempt was made by the Unions to extend them more widely. Even in large works the shop stewards were usually left to form, or not to form, Works and Workshop Committees, as they or the men in the works might choose. A good deal of pioneering work was going on ; but it was still quite experimental, and practically nothing was being done to co-ordinate the experiments made in different works or districts.

An idea of the degree of importance attached by the big Trade Unions to the workshop movement, even in such an industry as engineering, can be obtained from the wording of the rule under which, in the largest Union, the Amalgamated Society of Engineers, District Committees were empowered, but in no wise compelled, to appoint shop stewards before the war. Even this clause, as drafted, gives the impression of a higher degree of activity than actually existed ; for the A.S.E. had gone probably further than any other large Society towards the development of a shop steward system. Moreover, there were many districts in which the rule was not put into operation, and many others in which even the scanty duties attached to the office of steward were by no means regularly or completely performed. The rules of some of the smaller engineering Trade Unions contained provisions very similar to those which follow ; but in most cases the recognition, if any, accorded to the stewards was even more scanty. There was, then, hardly a hint in the pre-war developments of the position of importance and influence which the shop stewards' movement was before long to occupy in British Trade Unionism.[1]

[1] (a) Extract from pre-war rules of the Amalgamated Society of Engineers, as revised in 1913 (rule 15, clause 5 and part of clause 6) :

' (5) Committees may also appoint shop stewards in workshops or departments thereof in their respective districts, such stewards to be under the direction and control of the committee, by whom their duties shall be defined. The stewards shall report at least once each quarter on all matters affecting the trade, and keep the committee posted with all events occurring in the various shops, and they shall be paid 3s. for each quarterly report ; namely 2s. for duty performed, and 1s. for attendance and report to committee, these to be payable by the District Com-

CHAPTER III

WORKSHOP ORGANIZATION BEFORE THE WAR
(*continued*)

THE preceding chapter dealt entirely with workshop organizations originating with the workers themselves and more or less integrally related to their Trade Unions. But there was already in existence, before the war, a Works Committee movement of a different type, originating not with the workers, but with the employers. This movement also received a big impetus during the war period, as the result both of the rise of the shop stewards' movement and of the growth of what is usually known as ' Welfare Work '. It was also, as we shall see, the natural outcome of the methods by which it was sought to introduce dilution, and to alter workshop processes and organization, under stress of war conditions.

Workshop organization, when it originates from the employers' side, usually takes one or more of three distinct forms. Special representative committees elected by the workers are often established to look after the recreative, social, and welfare

mittees, and should a shop steward be discharged through executing his duties he shall be entitled to full wage benefit. If it is necessary for stewards to attend other meetings of the committee, they shall be remunerated the same as witnesses attending committee meetings.

' (6) District Committees shall also have power to call aggregate meetings, or shop meetings, upon trade questions.'

To this general rule the District Committees, where they took action, often added local ' Shop Stewards' Regulations ' of their own, and these were usually issued to the stewards as ' Instruction Cards ' by the more energetic districts. A provision, which practically always appeared in these local regulations, was added to the general rules in the revision which came into force in 1915. It was as follows :

' (*b*) Rules of A.S.E. as revised in 1915. This additional sentence to be added to Clause 5 in above.

The stewards shall be empowered to periodically examine the contribution cards of all members, and to demand that alleged members shall show their contribution cards for examination when starting work.'

aspects of the working of the establishment. For example, sports clubs are created and administered by committees elected by the employees ; the canteen, if any, is placed under the management of an elected Committee ; a provident fund is established, and a measure of self-government accorded to its membership ; or a special ' Welfare Committee ' is established, and consulted by the management in all matters, other than industrial questions dealt with by the Trade Unions, affecting the well-being of the workers. Committees of this type consist sometimes wholly of employees, and sometimes contain an element of appointed persons representing the management. They have as a general rule no organic connexion with the Trade Unions, and, in well-organized establishments, are usually precluded from dealing with industrial questions. They represent, for the most part, an attempt by the employer to make his works a real centre of social life, as well as a mere work-place, for his employees, and by this means not only to maintain health and reduce absenteeism but also to induce the workers to feel a keen sense of ' loyalty to the firm ', and, because of this loyalty, ' to put their best effort into their work.'

The second type of workshop organization originated by the employers is found mainly in those works which have adopted some form of co-partnership or profit-sharing. In these cases the workers often have either some special representation on the directorate or works management, chosen either by the whole body of employees, or, more often, by the select body of co-partners or profit-sharers among the employees. In other cases no direct representation on the directing or managing bodies is accorded ; but the workers are asked to create some sort of Advisory Committee of their own, and this Committee is consulted by the management on matters affecting the workers' interests. As this monograph does not profess to deal with profit-sharing or co-partnership, I shall have little to say of this form of workshop organization beyond the bare mention.

The third—and, from the standpoint of this study, by far

the most important—form of works organization originating from the employers' side is the type of Works or Workshop Committee or Council which is created definitely for the purpose of dealing with industrial questions. Bodies of this kind were not common in any industry in Great Britain before the war; but there were a considerable number of individual establishments in which they had been in existence in some cases for many years before 1914. There were important differences in character and aim among these Committees, which in no sense represented a coherent movement or a unity of purpose among the employers who called them into being. In some cases, as in certain important establishments in the biscuit industry, they were regarded, by the Trade Unions at least, as being primarily devices intended to keep the workers outside the ranks of the Unions, and to intensify and emphasize the sense of loyalty to the firm as against the idea of Labour solidarity. This was especially the case where employers' workshop organization of this ' industrial ' type was closely connected with a system of provident, sports, and welfare organization of the kind described above. There was a marked type of establishment, possessing a strongly entrenched system of representative committees and provident benefits of its own, in which before the war the Trade Unions found it very difficult to secure a firm hold.

On the other hand, there were also ' industrial ' Works Committees initiated by the employers in establishments which were strongly unionized; and these in a number of cases worked in full harmony with the Trade Unions, or at least not in definite antagonism to them. Works Committees consisting of representatives actually appointed by the workers on a Trade Union basis, i. e. representing each group of Union members in the works, were rare before the war; and the election was usually made by the whole of the workers in a particular grade or department. But the men chosen to serve might well be the workshop Trade Union leaders, and, in fact, the workers' side of the Committee might be equivalent to a fully representative body of Trade Union shop stewards.

The Works or Workshop Committees created by employers were, in the great majority of cases, joint bodies including, in addition to the members appointed by the wage-earning employees, a number appointed by the management, usually from heads of departments, works officials, and so on. Often a director, or the works manager, was chairman of the Committee. In the case of such joint bodies, there sometimes was, and sometimes was not, provision for separate meetings of the workers' side ; and, where such provision was made, the degree of independence shown by the workers' representatives tended to be greater. The secretary of the Committee was often a works official, provided and appointed by the management ; and the practice of having joint secretaries, one for each section of the joint Committee, had not been securely established, although it existed in a few cases.

Where the workers' side of one of these joint Committees possessed, or assumed, the right of independent meeting and of choosing its own officers, the result was sometimes that it became practically a separate committee, transacting apart its own business, and preparing the case for bringing forward the grievances of the workers. There might, in such a case, be very little difference between it and the type of Works Committee, mentioned in the previous chapter, which was created by the workers themselves. For a purely ' Workers' ' Committee of this type might hold either occasional or regular joint meetings with the management for purposes of discussion ; and clearly it might make little difference in practice whether, in theory, the workers' representatives formed a separate body or an organized ' side ' of a joint body.

Most of the forms of industrial works organization created by employers before the war were, however, largely ineffective. The workers, especially where they were organized, were often suspicious of them, even where they had been created by employers of undoubtedly good intention, who saw in them an indispensable aid to the softening of the growing—and, in their eyes, quite unnecessary and mistaken—antagonism between employers and workers. At the most, all that had been done in

Great Britain up to the time of the war was to make isolated experiments, which seemed most unlikely to lead to any considerable results. Even those few employers who had deliberately designed their workshop organization as a bulwark against the coming of Trade Unionism into their works were finding the defence increasingly precarious during the years of Labour unrest from 1910 to 1914 ; and some of them found their workers organizing in Unions, and the transformation of the workers' side of their cherished Works Committees into instruments of the Unions proceeding apace.

The great body of employers in Great Britain was entirely unaffected by any of these developments. Only a tiny minority of firms made any organized provision, beyond complying with the bare requirements of the Factory Acts, for ' welfare work '. Canteens were still exceptional ; and, although sports clubs and special works provident schemes were on the increase, the rate of development was slow. The lack of Trade Union organization on a works basis gave the ordinary employers no incentive to organize the labour personnel of the works, and the scientific study of workshop problems which has developed, for both good and ill, so greatly during the past few years, was quite unknown to the vast majority even of the big employers. Consequently, the firms which set out to establish any form of works organization were, for the most part, exceptional in attitude. Their motive was usually that of overcoming industrial unrest, either, as in the case of the more backward firms, by confronting Trade Unionism with a counter attraction, or, as in the case of the more advanced, by accepting Trade Unionism and endeavouring, by a limited acceptance, to overcome the developing antagonism between workers and employers.

The mere summary of the pre-war position contained in this and the preceding chapter is intended only to clear the ground for a study of the war-time development of the workshop movement. For the majority, both of employers and of Trade Unionists, that development was quite unexpected, and the experience of pre-war days, though it was carefully scanned, was found to afford but little guidance. In the munitions industries in particular, the war time conditions led irresistibly to a big development of the workshop movement; and it is mainly to the munitions industries that attention will necessarily be directed in this study. The metal trades have become, what the textile trades were in the early days of large-scale industrialism, the key group of capitalist industries, and the place of the most important new experiments in organization. They, more than any others, felt the brunt of war conditions; and it was natural that in them above all the new developments in workshop organization should take place.

CHAPTER IV

THE RISE OF THE WORKERS' COMMITTEES

In many respects the most remarkable development of
Labour organization during the war period was the growth
of the shop stewards' movement in the industries mainly
concerned in the production of munitions of war. It attracted
world-wide attention, and was written about, with more or
less understanding, by economists and journalists all over
the world. Moreover, although attention was concentrated
primarily upon its development in Great Britain, it was in fact
almost a world-wide phenomenon. Wherever the energies of
large bodies of men came to be concentrated on the production
of munitions of war, the shop stewards' movement, in one form
or another, and in one relationship or another to the Trade
Unions which were already in the field, made its dramatic
appearance.

This study deals only with the movement as it took place
in Great Britain. But, before the details are forgotten, some-
body ought to make the attempt to collect the materials for
a world-wide study of the development of workshop organization during the war period. Such an investigator would find
the pre-war German Trade Union system of ' workshop delegates ' undergoing a transformation in some respects parallel
to that of the ' shop steward ' in Great Britain : he would find
M. Albert Thomas, the French Minister of Munitions during
the most critical period, seeking to arrange with M. Merrheim,
of the Metal Workers' Federation, terms for the recognition
of a hastily improvised shop stewards' and workshop committee system : he would find a vigorous, but chaotic, growth
of Trade Union works committees in Italy. Everywhere,
similar conditions created developments which were largely
similar, although they differed in form according to the stage

of industrial development and Trade Union organization in the various countries.

In Great Britain, the causes for the rapid rise of the shop stewards' movement were mainly two. In the first place, for a variety of reasons the effect of the outbreak of war was to some extent to put out of action the ordinary methods of Trade Union bargaining. Even before emergency legislation restricting the use of the strike weapon began to be passed, it had become clear that Trade Union methods would necessarily undergo large modifications. Immediately after the declaration of war, the British Trade Union leaders proclaimed an ' industrial truce ' : strikes which were actually in progress were brought rapidly to an end, and the serious industrial troubles which were threatened for the autumn of 1914 were averted by the decision of the various Trade Unions to postpone for the time being their demands for higher wages and improved conditions of labour. These measures, however necessary or inevitable they may have been, put the machinery of Trade Unionism to some extent out of gear ; for at this stage no alternative methods to the normal forms of Trade Union action had been devised for dealing with grievances as they arose. Prices began immediately to rise, and the Unions, having decided to postpone their claims for improved conditions, found the standard of living of their members threatened by the increase in the cost of living. Despite the good resolutions of the Trade Union leaders, it was not long before there were again signs of a gathering storm of industrial unrest.

It must be remembered that the outbreak of war came at a time when the unrest in the ranks of British Labour was more serious and widespread than at any time since the rise of large-scale Trade Union organization. From 1911 onwards there had been a steady development of strike action ; and it seemed clear, in the summer of 1914, that the autumn was going to be a time of unprecedented industrial disturbance. Trouble was threatened in the railway, mining, engineering, building, and many other industries, and an active ' rank and file ' movement, keenly critical of the policy of the official

Trade Union leaders, had arisen, and was steadily gaining in strength. In the engineering industry in particular, this movement had created local machinery of its own in the various ' Amalgamation Committees ' which had sprung up in many of the principal centres throughout the country. Excluded from power in the official Trade Union organizations, the Amalgamation Committees had been actively proselytizing in the workshops, and had thus paved the way for the growth of workshop organization.

The first cause of the growth of the shop stewards' movement was thus the disarmament, partly compulsory and partly voluntary, of the official Trade Union movement in face of the international situation. The second, and active, cause was the existence of a big body of industrial unrest, and the partial mobilization of this unrest in organizations which were readily capable of assuming a workshop form. The actual spark which set the movement alight was the rise in prices, uncompensated, in face of the disarmament of the Trade Unions, by any effective official movement for a corresponding rise in wage rates.

These causes suffice to explain the origin of the war-time workshop movement; but they do not explain its rapid development, or the influence to which it attained during the war years. This was due to causes which had hardly begun to operate at the time when the movement originated, and, above all, to the immense changes in workshop practice which became necessary as the engineering and kindred industries were gradually adapted to the mass production of munitions of war. This cause operated, above all, in 1915 and 1916, and continued, though with slowly diminishing force, up to the end of the war period. During the latter years of the war there was added to it the intense friction which was created by the successive ' combings-out ' of the munition works for further ' man-power ' for the fighting forces, and by the restrictions in freedom and mobility of labour which the dwindling ' man-power ' of industry caused to be necessary. Thus, at every period of the war, from 1914 to the end of 1918, there were causes—sometimes one, and sometimes several—in operation, stimulating the growth of the workshop movement, and causing it to assume fresh functions, and arrogate to itself fresh authority, with every change in the conditions with which it had to deal.

There was no part of the industrial districts of Great Britain in which the ' left-wing ' groups within the Labour movement had obtained a stronger hold than upon the Clyde. The various Socialist Societies were there comparatively strong : Trade Unionism had reached a very high level of organization ; and the various ' rank and file ' bodies which were active during the period of unrest from 1910 to 1914 had done much of their most energetic propaganda in the industrial belt of Scotland. When the war broke out, the engineering Trade Unions upon the Clyde were engaged in an agitation for increased wages and improved conditions. This was set aside for the moment ; but soon the rise in the cost of living forced the issue again to the front. During the last months of 1914 negotiations took place between the Unions and the Clyde employers ; and the latter, taking advantage of a technicality, spun these out for a considerable time without allowing them to reach an issue. Finally, the matter was referred to a National Conference of the Engineering Employers' Federation and the Unions concerned, which was due to meet on the 12th of February.

By this time the delays had greatly accentuated the unrest, and the Shop Stewards' Committees in a number of the most important works initiated, as a protest against them, an embargo on overtime working, which was enforced in most of the important munition factories. Efforts to get this embargo removed failed, and it was in being when, on the 12th of February, the National Conference recommended the acceptance of a wage advance of $\frac{3}{4}d$. per hour instead of the men's demand of $2d$. and the Clyde employers' offer of $\frac{1}{2}d$. per hour. This joint recommendation had to be submitted to a ballot of the men concerned. Its rejection was from the first certain, and the men therefore saw in it only a device meant to ensure further delay. The Executive Councils of the Unions, however, were endeavouring to get the embargo on overtime removed at once, and favoured the acceptance of the offer because they feared that the dispute might retard the supply of munitions.

This position the workers on the Clyde refused to accept, and an unofficial strike broke out on the 16th of February, and spread rapidly. The strike movement was directed, not by the official Trade Union organizations in the Clyde area, but by a specially formed body, the ' Central Withdrawal of Labour Committee ' (or, as it was sometimes called, the ' Central Labour Withholding Committee ').

The origin of this Committee is in fact also the origin of the war-time Shop Stewards' Movement. The Clyde was among the areas in which, before the war, the Trade Unions had been the most active in securing that shop stewards should be generally appointed under the rules of the various Unions. They had formulated codes of working rules for stewards, and had allowed them to assume in the workshops some measure of delegated Trade Union authority. Moreover, there had come into existence, at various times before the war, unofficial and semi-official bodies based on the shop steward and workshop organization. Temporary ' Strike Committees ', called into being for the conduct of a particular dispute, had also sometimes, even before the war, been constituted largely on a workshop basis.

It was therefore not unnatural that, when in 1914 the workers on the Clyde desired to constitute an unofficial organization through which to press their claim for higher wages, they should do this by calling together delegates from the various engineering factories and workshops throughout the Clyde area. Many workshop meetings, convened for the most part by shop stewards in the various works, were held ; and as many as possible of the works were persuaded to send delegates to a central body, which was to co-ordinate and direct the whole movement. It is hardly to be supposed that most even of those who took the lead in forming the strike organization upon this basis realized that they were setting a definite new fashion in Trade Union combination, or that the body which they were creating was destined to exercise an influence going far beyond the dispute immediately in question, and far also beyond the Clyde.

It is true, however, that the form of organization adopted was by no means accidental. Among the Socialist organizations on the Clyde, an important place was held by the—numerically very small—Socialist Labour Party, which was an offshoot of the 'De Leonite' Socialist Labour Party in the United States. It happened that this party contained at the time a considerable sprinkling of the most active and intelligent of the younger Trade Unionists in the area, and that, in its industrial propaganda, great stress had always been laid on the importance of workshop organization as a means not only of more successful bargaining with employers, but also of obtaining that 'control of industry' on which the Socialist Labour Party, like other advanced schools of Socialist thought, then laid very much stress. The number of actual S.L.P. members among the shop stewards, and even among the men who were most active in forming the broader rank and file combinations, was at all times very small; but some of them had the great advantage of knowing precisely what they immediately wanted and of possessing a very considerable influence in the Trade Union movement locally.

The story of the Clyde strike of February 1915, of the intervention of the Government, of the threats of coercive measures against the strikers, and of the ultimate resumption of work when an award was made by a Government tribunal, the then newly constituted Committee on Production, cannot be told here. What is germane to this narrative is that the unofficial Central Withdrawal of Labour Committee, so far from being disbanded on the conclusion of the strike, decided to remain in being as a permanent body, and was reconstituted under the name of the 'Clyde Workers' Committee'.

The Clyde Workers' Committee remained in being throughout the war period. Its effective power fluctuated from time to time, and it was more than once re-formed in order that it might acquire a more fully representative character. Broadly speaking, however, it remained through all these changes much the same kind of body—a convention of delegates from the shop stewards and works and workshop committees throughout the Clyde area, appointing an Executive of its own quite distinct from the District Committees of the various Trade Unions to which its members belonged, and also from the District Committee of the Federation of Engineering and Shipbuilding Trades, the official Trade Union body concerned in co-ordinating the opinions and policies of the various Societies throughout the Clyde area.

There were in the engineering and kindred industries in the Clyde area a quite exceptionally large number of distinct Trade Union bodies, some of them branches of Unions which had their head-quarters in England, and some Scottish or purely local Societies. Most of the Societies organizing skilled workers were, in 1915, federated locally in the District Committee of the Engineering and Shipbuilding Trades Federation; but this body was weak, and in practice the separate Unions often took action on their own. The District Committees of the national organizations were, of course, subject and responsible to their various head offices, and a body which could promise to act on its own initiative, without recognizing the claims of the various head offices, was therefore in a position to make a strong local appeal. The Clyde Workers' Committee did not at any stage represent, either directly or indirectly, anything like the whole body of organized workers in the area. It was always the organization of a militant minority; but at times, when a particular grievance or agitation was very strongly felt, it was able successfully to wrest the leadership of the Clyde movement from the hands of the authorized Trade Union officials. This leadership was, however, as a rule somewhat precarious; and the Clyde Workers' Committee had carefully to watch its opportunity to place itself upon the crest of the wave of unrest, and to risk the loss of its influence if it failed at any time of action to carry the main body of Trade Union opinion with it.

The example of the Clyde speedily proved to be contagious. Largely under the influence of what had been accomplished by the Clyde workers, the Trade Unionists in other areas set busily about the stimulation and re-fashioning of the shop steward system, which in many districts had fallen almost into desuetude. In one district after another, not only were numerous additional stewards appointed : Workers' Committees of a more or less representative character were formed on the model of the Clyde Workers' Committee. Gradually, a Workers' Committee movement, based directly on the shop steward system, came into being in most of the important munitions centres, and played an important part in many areas in the industrial disturbances of the war years—for example, in the May strikes of 1917, the ' recognition ' strike of 1918, and the troubles arising out of the Military Service Acts.

It would be impossible, and also unprofitable, to write the history of this development, which continued, with varying fortunes, from time to time according to the changes in the industrial situation, throughout the war period. Many of the Committees were formed and re-formed again and again ; usually no clear records were kept, and no one troubled to chronicle the local activities of the various parts of the movement, except when they acquired for the moment a national importance on the occasion of some strike or other dislocation of industry for which they were held to be responsible. It is important, not to preserve the record of the vicissitudes through which each particular local body passed, but to get a general impression of the character and significance of the movement and of the general lines along which it developed. These were from the first largely similar in most of the areas affected, and they became more closely similar as the Workers' Committee movement gradually developed the skeleton of a separate national organization of its own, still wholly apart from the official organization of the Trade Union movement.

On the Clyde the movement spread rapidly from the time of its origin at the beginning of 1915. This was not, of course, the first occasion on which the workshops had been largely utilized as the basis of an emergency strike organization. What was new about the movement lay, in the first place, in the abnormality of the circumstances under which it came into being, and, secondly, in the possession by its leaders of certain new ideas of militant industrial policy. It was a commonplace, even before the war, with the young Socialists of the Clyde, organized in the Socialist Labour Party and in other left-wing organizations, that the established methods of British Trade Unionism were played out, and that the future would lie, in face of the growing concentration of industry, with ' all-grades ' mass organizations modelled on the American Industrial Workers of the World. The Socialist Labour Party had even endeavoured to persuade the workers to desert their ' craft ' Unions, and to re-organize on ' class ' lines in a new body, the Industrial Workers of Great Britain, which possessed some sort of skeleton organization. As long as this propaganda was directed to persuade men to leave the orthodox Trade Unions, it was inevitably ineffective, and met with hardly any response. But the ideas preached by the S.L.P. speakers were nevertheless bearing fruit, in that they were preparing the workers on the Clyde for more militant forms of industrial action.

During the war no more was heard of the I.W.G.B., but a great deal of the uselessness of orthodox Trade Union methods. The workers were called upon to organize for the deliberate purpose of assuming power in industry, and it was urged that the lines of craft division, which had so far prevented them from taking effective common action, must be broken down, and all classes of workers bound together in a great crusade against capitalism. The unity of organization among all workers employed in the same industry was a cardinal tenet, not only of the S.L.P. but also of many other advanced Trade Unionists, and this led naturally to the idea of a close bond of union among all the grades in any particular establishment.

Before the war most of the more advanced Trade Unionists were endeavouring to attain this object by the amalgamation of the existing Unions along industrial lines. Under the British law, especially as it stood up to 1917, stringent regulations were laid down governing the conditions under which

Trade Union amalgamations were allowed to take place. It was necessary to secure in favour of amalgamation a two-thirds majority, not merely of those voting, but of the whole member-ship of the Unions concerned. This was difficult enough to secure in normal times ; the outbreak of war, followed by the enlistment of a considerable percentage of Trade Unionists in the Army, made it almost impossible. The result was that the amalgamation movement was largely suspended, and the Trade Unionists who had been mainly active in it were free to turn their attention to other methods of promoting a militant industrial policy. Moreover, the causes which had been holding apart the amalgamationists on the one side and the advocates of the I.W.G.B. on the other largely disappeared. Both sections saw in the beginnings of the shop stewards' movement the rise of a new force making for ' all grades Unionism ' on aggressive class lines. The S.L.P. propagandists virtually abandoned their propaganda of what is known in America as ' dual Union-ism ', and concentrated on the development of a militant spirit in the workshops by fostering the ' all-grades ' tendencies inherent in the shop stewards' organization. Some of the members of the S.L.P. regarded this as merely the fore-runner of a new class organization which would speedily displace and replace the older Unions organized on ' craft ' lines ; other sections looked to it to hasten the amalgamation of the sectional Unions by bringing into being an effective spirit of workshop solidarity. The majority, no doubt, saw in it merely a con-venient instrument for the handling of the actual problems of the moment, and were content to use and develop it without seeking to give to their action a definite theoretical basis.

Elsewhere than upon the Clyde, the pre-war membership of the Socialist Labour Party was quite insignificant, and the idea of breaking away from the existing Trade Unions in order to form a new body on ' class ' lines had hardly been enter-tained. It was therefore only upon the Clyde that there was this definite confluence of previously divergent streams of opinion. In other areas the ' left wing ' elements in the Trade Unions were mostly ' amalgamationists ', and it was largely on the basis of the pre-war Amalgamation Committees that the shop stewards' and Workers' Committee movement was brought into being. The Amalgamation Committees, however, lingered on as separate bodies until 1918, when they were at last absorbed into the organization of the Workers' Committee movement.

The body of opinion strongly adverse to the existing leader-ship of the Trade Unions, which had grown up mainly between 1910 and 1914, formed the basis on which the new war-time movement was largely built. As we have seen, the progressive disarmament of official Trade Unionism under war conditions put powerful fresh arguments at the disposal of the ' rebel ' elements, and enabled them to make a far more successful and widespread appeal. This, however, could never have been done so effectively if the workshop had not offered an unrivalled, and also largely an unworked, field for militant industrial organization. If, as in Germany, the British Trade Unions had already before the war developed an extensive organization of their own in the factories, and seriously realized the possible strengthening of Trade Unionism which would result from Trade Union workshop representative machinery, it would have been far more difficult for an unofficial workshop move-ment to arise. It was the pre-war neglect of workshop problems by the Trade Unions, as well as the vast multiplication of such problems by war-time changes, that afforded the opportunity for the growth of a really vigorous ' left-wing ' workshop organization.

Thus, even where shop stewards had been appointed under the control of the Trade Union District Committees, we have seen that their powers and functions had been very limited in-deed, and that no considerable measure of recognition had been accorded to them. This jealousy of workshop bodies, and fear of giving them much scope for action, continued to a great extent during the war, and was naturally taken advantage of by the unofficial bodies, which organized the stewards and urged them to frame their policy, and take action, without much regard for the official attitude of the Trade Unions.

A rival allegiance, offering far greater powers than the Unions were willing to concede, was proferred to the shop stewards by the leaders of the Workers' Committee movement ; and, in times of crisis, the temptation to follow their lead was often irresistible.

At times it seemed as if the growth of the Workers' Committees would go far towards justifying the hopes or fears of those who saw in them a powerful potential rival and successor to the Trade Unions themselves, and as if a new kind of Unionism might actually base itself upon them. In fact, these hopes and fears were never realized. The movement remained a 'ginger' organization within the Trade Union movement, and led to no break away from its ranks. But it did go far, during the abnormal years of war, towards challenging the official Trade Union policy and ideals ; and, although its power was largely broken when the abnormal conditions of war gave place to the different abnormalities of the post-war period, it has undoubtedly left its permanent mark upon the structure and policy of the Trade Union movement, especially in the engineering and kindred industries, in which alone it attained to real strength during the war.

CHAPTER V

THE WAR-TIME SHOP STEWARD AND HIS WORK

In the second chapter of this study a general description has been given of the position and functions of those shop stewards who had been appointed to act on behalf of their Trade Unions before the war. It is now necessary to endeavour to describe the changes which came about in the position of the shop stewards under the very different conditions of war-time. This is by no means an easy task; for the situation differed from place to place, and many of the developments were never reduced to writing or expressed in any formal rules or codes. The shop stewards gained powers and functions as the changing situation thrust fresh tasks upon them, and as, either with or without the stimulus of a positive social theory, they themselves assumed fresh powers and responsibilities.

Before the war there was in any trade only one kind of shop steward, a minor workshop agent of the Trade Union or its District Committee. Usually this steward was chosen by the Trade Union members of his craft in the shop or department in which he worked, and his election had to be ratified by the Trade Union District Committee. Sometimes, the rules of the Union laid down certain qualifications, as to trade capacity, length of membership, &c., which a member must satisfy before he could become a steward; but in other cases there was no such stipulation. Sometimes, the District Committee issued to each duly appointed steward a special ' Shop Steward's Card ', authorizing him to inspect members' contribution books, and to undertake in the shop the other duties which might be assigned to him by the District Committee.

There was thus, even in theory, a good deal of elasticity as to the method of appointing shop stewards; but in practice the diversity was very much greater. The ratification by the District Committees of the elections made in the shops was frequently reduced to a mere form, and not seldom omitted altogether. The relations between the stewards and the District Committees were defined very loosely if at all; and in many areas the stewards in each works were practically left to devise their own methods of operation, and only came to the District Committees for support when actual trouble arose.

During the war years the activities of the various District Committees in promoting and authorizing the appointment of shop stewards very greatly increased, and Unions which had hitherto appointed no official stewards rapidly improvised some sort of workshop organization. But, side by side with these 'official' shop stewards, there grew up a new class of stewards, appointed by the workers in the shops to act on their behalf, but not authorized or confirmed in their appointment by any recognized Trade Union body. Sometimes these unofficial stewards were appointed by the members of a particular Union in a workshop; but in other cases the distinction between the various Unions was ignored, and stewards were appointed by all the workers, or by all workers of a particular trade or group, in a shop or department, without reference to the various Trade Unions in which they might be enrolled. In some instances even, there were in a single shop both official and unofficial stewards, claiming to represent the same groups of workers; and frequently unofficial stewards were appointed by those sections of the workers whom no official stewards could claim to represent. Often it was difficult, in a particular case, to say whether a given steward was unofficial or official; for in the absence, in many districts, of any formal rules governing appointments, there was often no clear line of division between the two groups.

In some areas a determined effort was made by the Trade Unions to bring order out of this chaos. In Coventry, where the development was most systematic and complete, the local Joint Committee of the Engineering Trade Unions took the whole business of appointing stewards out of the hands of the separate Unions, and itself issued stewards' credentials, accompanied by a definite set of regulations governing duties and procedure, on behalf of the Joint Committee as a whole.[1] In Coventry, thereafter, no steward represented a particular Union; but all were chosen to represent the whole of the workers in a particular shop or department, or section of a shop or department. There were, however, very few districts in which the Unions officially imitated the Coventry procedure; for in most areas the separate District Committees of the Unions refused to surrender the control of their stewards into the hands of a joint body.

There was, however, a very manifest need for common action among the numerous Unions in the engineering industry. In some instances these were craft Unions, representing a distinct trade or group of trades, and including within their ranks the whole of the organized workers in the trade or trades concerned. But in other cases, including the principal engineering grades, there were often several different Unions organizing largely the same classes of workers. For instance, the Amalgamated Society of Engineers, the Steam Engine Makers' Society, the Amalgamated Society of General Toolmakers, and the United Machine Workers' Association, all of which in 1920 joined forces with a number of smaller Societies to form the Amalgamated Engineering Union, were during the war distinct and largely overlapping bodies. The appointment of entirely separate sets of stewards to represent the members of each of these Unions resulted in a great duplication of work, and often meant that either a small group of workers belonging to a Union whose adherents were in a small minority in a particular establishment was left unrepresented, or that what was in reality a homogeneous group had to be represented by several different stewards, each responsible to his own distinct District Committee. The Amalgamated Society of Engineers, which was by far the largest Society, had naturally the most complete shop steward system; and the A.S.E. stewards, feeling strong enough to stand alone, often preferred to retain their separate identity and responsibility to their own Com-

[1] See Appendix A.

mittee, even when the less numerous stewards of the smaller Unions had been driven to take common action.

It was a further complication, that, as we have seen, the pre-war shop stewards were, in practically all cases, representatives of skilled workers. Despite the increase, during the earlier years of the twentieth century, in the numbers of the semi-skilled workers employed in engineering, these grades for the most part excluded from the ranks of the Unions of skilled workers, were very weakly organized, and had in most places attained to very scant powers of coherent action even where they were organized. As production was expanded during the war, there was, of course, an enormous influx of less skilled male and female labour into the engineering industry, and a high proportion of the newcomers gradually became organized. They were recruited, however, not by the Engineering Trade Unions, but by the ' General Labour ' Unions which enrolled the less skilled workers in all manner of industries and occupations. The Workers' Union, the National Union of General Workers, the National Federation of Women Workers and similar bodies increased vastly in membership during the war, and a very large part of the increase came from the less skilled workers in the munitions shops.

This process of organization was going on throughout the whole of the war period, and at the same time the mass of new industrial recruits, drawn from all manner of sources inside and outside industry, was gradually becoming more capable of coherent group action. Little by little these sections imitated the methods of organization which they found in vogue among the skilled workers in the shops in which they were employed. They too appointed their shop stewards, sometimes under the official auspices of the Trade Unions in which they were enrolled, and sometimes spontaneously, or under the influence of the unofficial Workers' Committee movement. Workshop organization among the less skilled workers never became anything like so complete or powerful as in the skilled trades ; but throughout the war period it was rapidly on the increase.

The relations between the stewards of the skilled workers

and those of the less skilled differed widely from district to district and often from shop to shop. Sometimes the two groups acted closely together ; sometimes there was practically no contact, or even a sharp antagonism, between them. Both the need for co-operation and the possibilities of antagonism increased with the development of the policy of ' dilution of labour ', which was officially promoted by the Government from 1915 onwards. On the whole, the degree of co-operation secured was far from satisfactory, and the less skilled workers remained throughout inadequately represented in the war-time shop stewards' movement.

While the number of stewards was thus rapidly increasing throughout practically the whole range of the munitions industries, their position and duties were also being rapidly transformed. The war-time steward, especially of the official variety, became to a large extent a negotiator on workshop grievances, a representative of the workers by whom he was appointed in dealing with foremen and with the management over all manner of workshop problems. The changes necessary to adapt the factories to war-time production, and to bring about the vast increase in output which was required, led to constant friction in the workshops, frequently over matters of apparently trivial importance, which might yet involve some vital Trade Union principle. More and more the shop stewards undertook the handling of these daily problems of workshop administration, calling in the Union officials only when they were unable to bring about a direct settlement by formal or informal negotiation.

These increasing functions necessarily led to a further stage in the development of workshop organization. It was not enough for a particular steward to take up the grievances of the small group of workers whom he directly represented, or even for informal co-operation to be arranged as it was required by the various stewards in a department, shop, or works. It became more and more necessary for all the stewards to act in regular co-operation, and to devise a common organization within each department, and for each establishment as a whole.

Consequently, Shop Stewards' Committees, Workshop Committees, and Works Committees, all alike based on the shop steward system, began to develop on a considerable scale. Usually the stewards in a particular shop appointed from their own number a secretary or convener, who had power to call meetings of all the stewards in the shop. Sometimes these stewards then appointed a Committee to act with the convener. Either the Committee, or the whole body of stewards, could convene at any time a workshop meeting, which all the workers in the shop, or at least all those represented by the stewards' organization, were invited to attend. Workshop meetings of this type had been held before the war when a grievance had arisen, or when a District Committee wished to discuss some question with the workers in a particular shop; but they increased very greatly under pressure of war conditions, and a good deal of trouble arose in certain cases when the stewards convened works meetings frequently in the firm's time.

In the large establishments, consisting of a number of considerable shops or departments, organization did not stop short at a single shop. An inclusive body was often constituted to represent the Trade Unionists in the works as a whole. Sometimes the conveners from each of the shops were appointed, usually by a meeting of all the stewards in the establishment, to form a Works Committee, and sometimes other directly elected representatives sat with them on the Committee. In these cases it was usual also to appoint a convener of shop stewards, and perhaps a Chairman of Committee, for the works as a whole.

The head convener of shop stewards in the big establishments became in many cases a very important person in the direction of war-time Trade Union policy; and, as we shall see, considerable friction arose, in some instances, between the workers and the management as to the measure of recognition to be accorded to him. Where the stewards' organization was strong, the head convener claimed the right to enter any department in the works for the purpose of obtaining information or dealing with grievances as they arose. When a shop steward found himself confronted with a problem which he could not settle himself with the foreman, or which he considered to involve a principle of importance to other sections of workers in the establishment, he would, as a rule, send for the convener of his department. The convener in turn, if he could not deal with the case or felt it to be vital, would similarly send for the head convener for the works as a whole. In one form or another, the majority of the big establishments were gradually brought to recognize the head convener's right to deal with grievances arising in departments other than his own, and to accord to him at least a limited right of access to all departments. But there was much friction in the establishment of the principle, and one of the most important engineering disputes of the war period, the strike at Parkhead Forge on the Clyde in March 1916, centred largely round the question whether the head convener, David Kirkwood, had or had not the right to enter a particular department in the performance of his functions as head steward of the works.

Often, the practice of allowing the stewards and head stewards certain special immunities from workshop discipline in order to enable them to perform their functions as representatives of the workers grew up silently, and without any attempt, on either side, at formal definition. Then friction often arose when a particular steward was held by the management, or by his foreman, to have exceeded these purely customary and undefined limits of action, or when a practice, which the workers had considered as securely established, was suddenly challenged by a foreman or by order of the management as a whole. When any attempt was made to agree formally upon the scope of shop stewards' duties and privileges, the right of access to other departments for the head stewards, and the right of stewards generally to leave their work for the purpose of dealing with cases arising within their jurisdiction, were seldom admitted absolutely by the management, which often endeavoured to lay down a code of rules to be observed.[1]

[1] See Appendix B, ' Regulations governing activities of Shop Stewards ', issued by Hans Renold, Ltd.

Formal definition proved, however, in practice very difficult, and the usual method of meeting the difficulty was by a liberal ' give and take ' on both sides.

Of course, one of the determining factors which enabled the shop stewards' movement so rapidly and successfully to secure, without formal recognition by the employers' associations, so much actual power and recognition from the management of the various works was the very great shortage of skilled workers. Each firm knew that, if it lost its existing complement of skilled workers, it would find replacement difficult, if not impossible. Each firm was therefore anxious to retain its skilled men, and willing, with that object, to tolerate a degree of independence which the workers could certainly not have secured so readily under any other circumstances.

It must not, however, be supposed that anything like a uniform procedure or system of *de facto* recognition of the shop stewards' organization was established. The position varied from works to works and from district to district, according to the attitude of the management, the temper and leadership of the shop stewards themselves, the state of organization, the position on the District Committees of the Unions, and many other factors down to mere chance. In the works the stewards might enjoy a privilege, the right to which was hotly disputed in the works next door, while, in relation to some other privilege, the position might be reversed. The whole development was empirical, and it was not until the last year of the war that any attempt was made to standardize it on national lines.

Unlike the full-time Trade Union officials, but like the majority of the district officers of the Unions, practically the whole of the shop stewards were men actually working at their trades, as well as performing their duties as works representatives. In a very few cases a single steward in a works was, indeed, relieved of the necessity of working at his trade, and either paid wages by the firm while he was engaged as a shop steward, or reimbursed for his lost earnings by a levy upon the workers in the establishment. But, even where the steward continued to work at his trade, as he usually did, he inevitably lost a larger or smaller number of hours' work a week while he was engaged on his duties as a steward. Here, again, his wages were sometimes made up by the firm, and sometimes he was reimbursed for his lost time by his fellow-workers. Keen Trade Unionists as a rule preferred the latter method, because they held that it gave the stewards a greater measure of independence in their dealings with the management. The number of stewards who devoted anything like their full time to their duties as stewards always remained small; and the great majority continued to work at their trades for the greater part of the week. It seems to be clear that most men who undertook the duties of shop stewards lost money by doing so.

In all these processes of growth which I have been describing, both the official and the unofficial shop stewards shared. Naturally, as the power of the workshop organizations grew, the measure of *de facto* recognition accorded to them by the Trade Unions also increased. The meetings between District Committees and their shop stewards, which had been occasionally held before the war, became more regular and important, and the reports made to the District Committees by the stewards on workshop developments were increasingly attended to, and made the basis of official Trade Union action. There was still, especially among the older men among the Trade Union leaders, considerable suspicion of the new powers acquired by the workshop bodies; and the danger that district and national Trade Union customs and regulations would be undermined by workshop bargaining was freely pointed out. But more and more the Trade Union District Committees tended to pass under the control of younger men, who had often themselves been shop stewards, and were keen on the utmost possible development of workshop organization within the bounds of the official Trade Union movement. The principal difficulties between the District Committees and the shop stewards occurred during the earlier stages of ' dilution '; and, when these had been surmounted, the two forms of organization tended to work far more smoothly together, and opposition was largely confined to the relations between the District Committees and the unofficial and militant ' Workers Committees ' described in the preceding chapter. Thus, during the later years of the war, the official organization of shop stewards had come to be regarded, almost everywhere, as an integral part of local Trade Union machinery ; and the Unions in practice allowed the stewards, and the Works and Workshop Committees constituted by them, considerable freedom of negotiation as long as actually established district or national standards of wages and conditions of employment were not interfered with. The shop stewards and committees came to serve as an exceedingly useful first line of Trade Union defence, and also enabled the Unions to deal with many matters which they would have been quite unable to tackle without a special organization in each workshop or factory in which their members were employed. This led finally to the attempt to stabilize and standardize the shop stewards' organization by collective agreement on a national scale, as an officially recognized part of the machinery of Trade Unionism throughout the engineering and kindred industries. But before we deal with the negotiations between the Trade Unions and the engineering employers which led up to the shop stewards' agreements of 1917 and 1919, it is necessary to obtain a closer view of the actual achievements of the workshop organizations during the war, by studying them in close relation to some of the most important particular groups of problems with which they attempted to deal.

CHAPTER VI

THE SHOP STEWARDS AND DILUTION

BEFORE the end of 1914 the problem of labour shortage was already beginning to present itself in one or two branches of the munitions industries, especially in the manufacture of shells and fuses. Negotiations between the Trade Unions and the Engineering Employers' Federation resulted in the Shells and Fuses Agreement, signed on the 5th of March 1915, under which the first measure of dilution was introduced. From the date of appointment of the Committee on Production (the 2nd of February 1915), the Government itself took an active part in promoting the dilution [1] of labour by the relaxation of Trade Union rules and the introduction of less skilled male and female workers. The Treasury Conferences of the 17th to 19th of March, and the 25th of March 1915, over which Mr. Lloyd George presided, resulted in the giving by the Trade Unions of a general assent to necessary measures of dilution, subject to guarantees as to the rates to be paid and as to the restoration of suspended Trade Union regulations at the conclusion of the war. In June and July the substance of the 'Treasury Agreement' was embodied in the first Munitions of War Act, which was passed into law on the 2nd of July. This Act for the first time provided the Government with compulsory powers for the introduction of dilution on any scale that might be required. In the autumn of 1915 the Government issued its general Dilution Scheme, based on reports made to the Ministry of Munitions by the Central Labour Supply Committee, on which Trade Unions and employers' associations were represented side by side with the

---

[1] 'Dilution'—that is, the introduction of less skilled workers to undertake the whole or a part of the work previously done by workers of greater skill or experience, often, but not always, accompanied by simplification of machinery, or the breaking up of a job into a number of simpler operations.

Government departments concerned in the production of munitions. The famous ' L ' Circulars,[1] in which the regulations for the introduction of the scheme were embodied, laid down not only the rates to be paid, but also a recognized procedure for workshop consultations on the occasion of introducing dilution into any establishment. From the autumn of 1915 onwards, dilution was constantly being extended, as the demand for munitions became greater and the shortage of workers more acute.

Considering the rate of progress in the introduction of dilution to be too slow, the Ministry of Munitions, in January 1916, appointed two special Dilution Commissions, one for the North-East Coast, or Tyne, area, and the other for the Clyde area. The Commissioners were instructed to go round the various workshops in these areas and to take steps for the introduction of further measures of dilution wherever they felt that it could be usefully extended. The Commissioners first visited the local Trade Union bodies and employers' associations and endeavoured to reach agreement with them as to their general lines of procedure. They then, taking a single works at a time, made a full inspection, entered into negotiations with the management and with representatives of the workers in the establishment, and drew up for each works a special Dilution Scheme, including full details of the processes on which less skilled labour was to be introduced, the rates to be paid, the measure of recognition to be accorded to shop stewards and Trade Union representatives in the working of the scheme, and so on. Subsequently, the Tyne Commission was disbanded, and the remaining work handed over to the Clyde Commissioners, who also installed a Dilution Scheme at Barrow-in-Furness on much the same lines. When this initial work was done, the Clyde Commission too was disbanded, and the work of promoting the extension of dilution

---

[1] ' L ' Circulars, i. e. circulars dealing with labour conditions, issued by the Ministry of Munitions to establishments controlled under the Munitions of War Acts. The procedure under which ' dilution ' was introduced is fully described in the companion study in this series, *Trade Unionism and Munitions.*

was thereafter carried on by the regional officers of the Ministry of Munitions, or, in the shipbuilding centres, by the corresponding officers of the Admiralty Shipyard Labour Department.[1]

Necessary as it was for the avoidance of constant friction with the Trade Unions to lay down precise and nationally applicable regulations governing the conditions under which the substitution of less skilled workers in the munitions industries could take place, dilution was, and remained throughout the war period, essentially a workshop problem. However precisely the national conditions might be formulated, there remained inevitably countless points of detail which had to be adjusted separately for each works or department. General regulations for the introduction of dilution were found either to remain inoperative, or to serve as a source of constant friction, unless a definite procedure was laid down for applying their provisions to each individual case. The consciousness of this fact, and the certainty that dilution would prove effective only when it was introduced with the consent, and, if possible, the willing co-operation, of the skilled workers affected, were the causes which led to the appointment of the Dilution Commissioners for the Clyde and Tyne. And, as soon as the Commissioners faced up to their problem, they realized that they could only achieve real results if they went directly to the organized workers in the shops and endeavoured to fix up with them agreements as to the conditions under which dilution might be introduced or extended. Sometimes the district and national officers of the Trade Unions were inclined to take exception to this procedure, on the ground that agreements made directly between the Commissioners and the workshop organizations might be so drawn as to undermine established district conditions, and, by introducing arbitrary variations from shop to shop, destroy the minimum district standards which it had been the main work of the Unions to stabilize and compel the employers to accept. Both on the Clyde and

[1] For a fuller account of the development of war-time dilution in the British munitions industries, see the companion study to this monograph, *Trade Unionism and Munitions.*

on the Tyne, difficult cases arose in which workshop agreements in violation of district conditions were made by the Commissioners ; but, with experience, this difficulty was largely avoided, and most of the works agreement were so drawn as to be consistent with the district Trade Union regulations, or, if they involved a departure from them, were submitted to the District Committees concerned before ratification by the workshop bodies.   There were, indeed, constant disputes arising out of the failure of employers to comply with the recognized practice of consulting the workers upon any proposed measures of dilution ; but, here again, as the shop stewards' organization grew in strength, regular forms of consultation tended to be developed.   Dilution was, however, often introduced in particular cases in face of Trade Union or workshop opposition ; for, behind the recognized machinery for consultation and negotiation, were the coercive powers exercised by the Ministry of Munitions under the Munitions of War Acts of 1915 and the following years.

The work of the special Clyde and Tyne Dilution Commissioners, and the to some extent similar procedure adopted by the Ministry of Munitions in other areas, exercised a very important influence on the development of the workshop movement.   As it came more and more to be realized that even the most water-tight scheme of dilution could in practice be rendered useless by workshop opposition, it came to be recognized as a matter of the first importance to secure workshop co-operation.   Naturally, the opposition to any form of dilution was, as a rule, keenest in those cases in which firms endeavoured to introduce or extend it without any consultation with the workers whose duties and remuneration it was bound to affect. The better organized firms, and the more far-seeing officers of the Ministry of Munitions, therefore endeavoured, wherever possible, to secure for their measures the assent of the shop stewards as well as of the national and local Trade Union officials.   Had this been done more generally, and had all officers of the Ministry of Munitions and all employers consistently pursued this policy, there is no doubt that a very great deal of friction which actually occurred would have been eliminated, and the work of introducing dilution far more rapidly and successfully carried through.

Whatever the attitude of the Ministry and of the employers might be, the effect of the coming of dilution was almost everywhere a great increase in the strength and importance of the shop stewards and of the workshop bodies based upon them. Where they were fully consulted, as in the majority of cases on the Clyde and Tyne, considerable administrative and negotiating functions fell upon the stewards, who had both to agree upon the detailed conditions for the application of the general principles laid down, and to watch at every stage the actual working of the Dilution Schemes, taking up all difficulties and disputes as they arose, and endeavouring to forestall trouble by being beforehand with each grievance. Where consultation was absent or defective, the duties which fell upon the stewards were different, but certainly not less extensive. They had to keep a watch on all developments, and to report to their organizations upon all attempts to introduce ' diluted labour ', to readjust processes, or to lower wage rates or threaten established Trade Union customs. According to their character and attitude, they might be reporting either to the District Committee of their Trade Union, or to the local unofficial Workers' Committee, or to both. In case of serious grievances, they might easily find themselves, even despite the law applying compulsory arbitration for the war period, engaged as ' rank and file ' leaders in an unofficial strike.

From 1915 to 1917 at least, the introduction and extension of dilution were certainly the most powerful factors in promoting the development of the shop stewards' movement, and in securing for the stewards, and for their Works and Workshop Committees, a degree of recognition from the employers and from the Government which they would otherwise have found it very difficult to achieve. Moreover, the need for dilution strengthened the shop stewards, not only in their dealings with the employers and with the divisional and local officers of the Ministry of Munitions and the Admiralty, but also in relation to their own members. During those years some fresh measure of dilution, some change in process or in the grade of labour operating a particular machine, was constantly being made. Dilution came, not as a sudden and complete sweeping away of one system in the workshops in favour of another, but as a long series of piece-meal changes, often affecting at a particular moment only a small group, or even an isolated worker. Consequently, the shop stewards were kept always busy. As soon as they had settled the case of the substitution of half a dozen semi-skilled workers for skilled tradesmen on as many capstan or turret lathes in one part of the shop, their attention would be engaged by a proposal to employ women on a grinding, or milling, or boring machine. As soon as that was settled, a case would arise in which the management proposed the sub-division of a particular process, and the handing over of part of it to an unskilled worker operating an automatic machine. Questions as to the price to be paid, under the war-time guarantees safeguarding piece-work rates on diluted processes, arose all day and every day. All this made the individual worker far more dependent on his shop steward than under the normal, and comparatively unvarying, conditions of workshop practice, and called, on the steward's side, for unceasing vigilance and readiness to deal with any cause of friction.

The shop stewards' organization had to be improvised, for the most part, very much in a hurry in order to deal with this rapidly developing situation. The number of stewards had to be doubled, trebled, quadrupled, in a few weeks. Consequently the men who became shop stewards were of very unequal degrees of ability, tact, and resource. It was impossible, in improvising an organization with such speed, to secure that the best men available should be always chosen, or to prevent a large number of bad mistakes from being made. Often the best men were unwilling to push themselves forward, and the shop stewards at first selected were, in many cases, no more than a ' scratch team '. Moreover, the job itself was still in the making ; and there was no very clear idea of the nature and extent of the duties which it would involve. Very little advice or assistance was forthcoming from the national or district officers of the Trade Unions ; and the stewards, for the most part, were left to settle down as best they might, and to make their own place by the actual manner in which they handled each situation as it arose. In the absence of official guidance, it is not surprising that the unofficial ' left-wing ' organizations, whose leaders much more rapidly and fully apprehended the possibilities of the workshop movement, gained a wide influence even over stewards who had had no previous contact with their revolutionary point of view. The political consequences of this ' left-wing ' domination are dealt with in a later chapter of this study ; its immediate industrial consequence was, on the whole, to give the shop stewards a conception of their office as one of the means to the gaining of ' workers' control ' in industry, and to make them envisage the problems of dilution as part of the bigger problem of the transformation of production under the influence of large-scale capitalist organization.

To say this is not to suggest that the great mass of the shop stewards ever became revolutionaries or even Socialists in any theoretical sense. The greater part of the time occupied by their duties was spent in dealing with comparatively detailed points of workshop readjustment, which afforded little scope for the introduction of revolutionary ideas. The stewards of the skilled trades were largely concerned in preventing unregulated dilution, and in safeguarding, as far as possible, the position of the tradesmen wherever dilution was introduced or extended. The stewards of the less skilled workers were active both in securing reasonable payment and conditions for their members who were called upon to undertake skilled or semi-skilled work, and in pushing the claims of the less skilled grades to a freer entry into occupations within which the skilled trades claimed a monopoly. Although, therefore, there was, on many matters of general concern, a common point of view and solidarity among all the grades of workers in the shops, there were not a few questions, especially among those which

arose directly out of dilution, which tended to range the
stewards of the skilled and less skilled trades on opposite sides.
The test of really effective workshop organization lay, throughout
the war period, largely in the extent to which the stewards of
the various grades succeeded in settling their differences among
themselves and so avoided the exploitation of their occasional
opposition by the management.

For the most part, the shop stewards, except at moments
of abnormal excitement, usually contented themselves with
doing, to the best of their power, the actual jobs which presented themselves in the ordinary course of their workshop
activities. If women or unskilled men were ' upgraded ' and
set to perform an operation hitherto executed by labour of
a higher grade, they set themselves to secure reasonable rates
of wages and piece-work prices, to get defined by agreement
with the management the payment and status of the supervisors or tool-setters who were necessary to look after the
' dilutees ', and to procure the fullest possible guarantees that
all trade customs suspended as a consequence of dilution would
be restored on the termination of the war. Although the shop
stewards' movement rose to fame primarily as a quasi-revolu-
tionary movement, the great mass of the work done by the
stewards remained throughout the war period of this essentially
unrevolutionary character.

There can be no doubt that, on the whole, the existence of
comparatively strong workshop organization in most branches
of the munitions industries enabled dilution to proceed more
smoothly than it would otherwise have done. It is true that
the shop steward system was often felt by employers as a barrier
to forms of dilution which they desired to introduce, and that
the stewards did often vigorously oppose particular measures
of dilution which the employers desired. It is true also that,
if the workers had merely allowed the employers to introduce
as much dilution as they might choose how and when they
liked, the process of dilution would have been far smoother
than it actually was. This, however, was never really a possibility. The alternative to the regulation of the processes of

dilution by the shop stewards would have been an indiscriminate mass opposition in the workshops to dilution in all its forms; and opposition of this sort would have led to far greater friction, and made the carrying through of dilution in practice involve far more difficulty, than were actually experienced at any stage. It was where a particular employer attempted to ignore the workshop movement, or to victimize its leaders, or where measures of dilution were put into effect without prior consultation, that the greatest amount of unrest developed, and strikes were most likely to occur.

The almost hourly problems arising out of dilution in every big establishment were largely instrumental, during the earlier years of the war, in setting the shop stewards' organization firmly on its feet, and in bringing about its development from the stage when the stewards of each trade and shop remained more or less isolated, to the stage when Workshop and Works Committees, with duly appointed conveners, in close touch with similar bodies in other establishments, became a regular feature of factory organization. But, especially during the later years of the war, important fresh influences came into play. Of the purely industrial problems, the most important during this period was the widespread attempt to introduce ' payment by results '. Of politico-economic problems, those which principally affected the workshop movement were, first, the military conscription introduced in 1916, and secondly the economic consequences of compulsory military service— the various issues which were hotly debated under the name ' industrial conscription '. We must now turn to a study of the influence of these questions on the workshop movement.

CHAPTER VII

PAYMENT BY RESULTS IN THE WORKSHOPS

THE engineering and kindred industries were, before the war, conducted partly on the piece-work and partly on the time-work system of wage payment. Time-work, on the whole, still predominated among the skilled workers, while the majority of the less skilled machine-workers on repetition processes were remunerated on a piece-work basis. The premium bonus system, under which the worker receives, in addition to his time-rate, a bonus for time saved out of the time allowed for doing the job, was on the increase, and had been extensively adopted by a few big firms. As a rule, the skilled time-workers in the industry were determined to maintain the time-work system, and were strongly hostile to the introduction of payment by results in any form. Those workers who were actually employed on piece-work or bonus systems were divided in their attitude ; but the more active Trade Unionists in the industry were, for the most part, strongly in favour of time-work.

As we have seen, the system theoretically in operation for the fixing of piece-work prices was that of ' mutuality ', or individual bargaining between the workman who was to do the job and the foreman or rate-fixer. This was the procedure laid down in the successive national engineering agreements which were in force from 1897 to 1914, when the Amalgamated Society of Engineers terminated the agreement signed in 1907. At the time of the outbreak of war, the greater part of the industry was carrying on without a written agreement, and the conclusion of a new agreement was under discussion.

The position of workers under the premium bonus system was somewhat ambiguous. In some cases at least, the employers took the view that the granting of the bonus was a purely gratuitous or *ex gratia* action on their part, and that either collective or individual bargaining about the amount of the bonus, or the basis on which it was calculated, would be out of place. In a few cases the Trade Unions reached the same conclusion from an opposite point of view. In certain time-work trades, such as pattern-making, in which the Unions insisted in theory on a rigid adherence to the time-work system, they yet found it inexpedient to withdraw their members from shops in which the employers insisted on applying the premium bonus system. In these cases they issued instructions to their members to continue working as if the sole basis of payment were the time-work basis, and to refuse to enter into any discussion with the management concerning the amount or method of calculating the bonus. If, in face of this attitude, the employer persisted in adding a bonus payment to the weekly time-wage, that, it was held, was no concern of the Trade Union.

In practice, as we have seen, the methods of fixing and adjusting piece-work prices and other forms of remuneration under payment by results varied widely from case to case. In some instances the employer fixed prices at will, and the workers, without examining individual prices, had regard only to the aggregate of their weekly earnings, and lodged a general complaint if they considered this to be inadequate. In other cases, ' mutuality ', modified by a measure of informal joint action among the workers of the same trade in the shop, was actually in operation ; in yet others, more or less complete and recognized forms of collective workshop bargaining had been developed. ' Scientific Management ', or any attempt to fix prices on the basis of an accurate study of times and motions, was only in operation in a very few establishments, and was generally disliked by employers as much as by workers. Usually, where systems of payment by results were in operation, prices or basis times were fixed on a purely empirical basis, or frequently even by mere guess work.

The result was that in very many cases the piece-work prices offered or times allowed bore only a very distant relationship to the amount of work actually required for the performance of the operations concerned. It was often urged, by employers as well as by workers, that this did not matter, because, if one price was too low, another was too high, and, in the result, the whole of the prices averaged out more or less fairly. So far as the actual amount of earnings under normal conditions was concerned, this may indeed have been largely the case; for, in the absence of any agreed price-lists, the foremen and rate-fixers were often in a position, by manipulating prices and jobs, to make earnings work out practically at what level they chose. It is true that the employers had agreed not to alter a piece-work price except when some change in the process or method of manufacture took place; but it is clear that such minor changes were often made with the sole object of altering the price, and, on jobbing work, a fresh price had often to be fixed for practically each job or group of operations. Moreover, even where prices were left untouched, the foreman could usually bring out the earnings of each worker more or less at the desired level by a little attention to the distribution of the work so as to give each man the approved proportion of ' fatly ' or ' leanly ' priced jobs.

When a piece-work price was being fixed, the object of the management was that of finding the shortest possible time in which it could be done, while that of the men was to take long enough in the doing of it to ensure that, on future occasions, it would always allow the worker to earn a good piece-work balance. Moreover, when a job was highly priced, the workers felt that, if they did it in the least possible time, and so made high earnings, the only result would be that the management would find some way of ' cutting ' the price, or of balancing the account by fixing the prices for other operations at a correspondingly low level. The employer, therefore, usually ' speeded up ', and the workers usually ' speeded down '. The result was a widespread prevalence, in shops working on systems of payment by results, of mutual antagonism, ' speeding up ' and ' ca' canny ', which often more than neutralized the incentive to increased output which the piece-work system was designed to provide.

The degree in which these practices prevailed varied a great deal from shop to shop ; but the results of the inquiries into the operation of piece-work systems which were held during the war under the auspices of the Ministry of Munitions were sufficiently startling. A full inquiry into piece-work conditions in the Manchester area, for example, revealed in 1917 all the practices referred to above in full swing in a large number of reputable establishments. The war, however, introduced over a considerable part of the productive field new factors which largely affected the position. When the Trade Unions agreed, in March 1915, to remove all restrictions on production and to admit dilution in principle, they secured the concession that piece-work prices should be maintained. Clause 5 of the Treasury Agreement, afterwards incorporated in the Munitions Act of 1915 as paragraph 5 of Schedule II, gave this pledge in the following terms :

> The relaxation of existing demarcation restrictions or the admission of semi-skilled or female labour shall not affect adversely the rates customarily paid for the job. In cases where men who ordinarily do the work are adversely affected thereby, the necessary readjustments shall be made so that they can maintain their previous earnings.

The drafting of this clause is obviously ambiguous, and a great deal of trouble subsequently arose as to its interpretation. The intention was, however, clearly to prevent the introduction of less skilled, and therefore ordinarily lower-paid, classes of labour from being used as a reason for the reduction of any established piece-work price.

Actually, prices were in many cases reduced ; but, where they were not, curious anomalies sometimes arose. The effect of the guarantee against reductions was to remove the immediate reason for ' ca' canny ', and, the need for increased production for war purposes adding a fresh incentive, output on certain operations went up to an amazing extent, in the case both of skilled and of less skilled substitute workers. In one way or another, employers often devised ways of ' cutting ' these prices, and a good deal of friction occurred in consequence. A further anomaly soon appeared. When the shortage of labour led to an extension of dilution from the comparatively simple repetitive operations, such as shell, fuse, and cartridge-case making, on which it was first introduced, to more complex processes ordinarily performed by fully skilled men, the tendency was naturally to take away from the skilled men the simpler, and therefore more easily diluted, parts of their work, and to hand these over to less skilled workers, leaving to the craftsmen only those parts of their ordinary work which absolutely necessitated a high degree of skill. Now, as a rule, the ' fattest ' jobs from the point of view of earning capacity were also the simplest. Accordingly, the fully skilled craftsmen found the more paying part of their work taken away from them and ' diluted ', while they were left with the least paying, though doubtless the most interesting, jobs.

Piece-work prices having been, to some extent at least, stabilized at the pre-war level, this meant that the less skilled dilutees who took over these jobs often found themselves able to earn more than the fully skilled craftsmen—a position which was an endless source of friction. Gradually, this situation was dealt with, despite the guarantees incorporated in the Treasury Agreement and the Munitions Act, by the cutting down, under one pretext or another, of many of the prices which yielded the highest earnings ;[1] but it was the main cause of the granting of the special 12½ per cent. bonus to skilled workers in 1917, the extension of which to other grades led to such confusion during the earlier months of 1918.

All these factors, and the other alterations involved in the adaptation of peace-time systems of payment by results to the different conditions prevailing when the character of the product was changed in order to meet the war demands, afforded occupation for shop stewards, and helped to further the development of workshop organization. In addition to watching over dilution questions in the more restricted sense, the shop stewards and committees were constantly dealing with problems arising out of the fixing and adjustment of piece-work

[1] For a fuller discussion of this problem see my companion study, *Trade Unionism and Munitions*.

prices. When the right to consultation over questions of dilution was admitted, it was almost impossible not to recognize the right of the workers to employ the method of collective bargaining in relation to piece-work prices and even premium bonus basis times ; for these often had a direct bearing on the effect of the measures of dilution that were being introduced. Consequently, there was a steady tendency, throughout the war period, towards an increased recognition of the workers' right to bargain collectively, instead of individually, concerning piece-work prices, and the more active shop stewards' Committees played an increasing part in such bargaining, and tended more and more to enter into direct workshop agreements with the management for the regulation of the conditions under which systems of payment by results were operated.

This process became more marked as the war continued, and to it were added, during the latter war years, important fresh factors. The great mass of the diluted labour introduced, during 1915 and 1916, on the simpler repetitive processes of munitions production was employed under some form of payment by results ; usually, during the earlier period, under the piece-work system. But it was not until 1917, when the shortage of skilled labour had become very acute, that any considerable attempt was made, on a national scale, to apply payment by results to large sections of the skilled time-workers in the engineering and shipbuilding industries. The tendency from 1914 to 1916 was indeed all in the direction of an increasing substitution of payment by results for time-work ; but, during those years, the encroachments on time-work were only made in isolated establishments, and did not rouse violent Trade Union opposition on a national scale. The Government departments, however, more and more accepted the view of the employers, who had long desired to bring about a great extension of payment by results, and, towards the end of 1916, the Government decided to launch a national campaign with the object of securing the removal of all obstacles placed by the Trade Unions in the way of the universal adoption of the system.

To this the Unions, very many of whose members were invincibly opposed to payment by results, would in no wise agree. Encountering keen opposition, the Government endeavoured to persuade the Unions to enter into an inquiry with the object of ascertaining how far, and under what conditions, the system could be extended ; but the proposal to enter into this inquiry was rejected after a special conference had been held between the Unions and representatives of the Government in January 1917. The Government, however, by no means abandoned its efforts. From the beginning of 1917 onwards, the divisional and local officers of the Ministry of Munitions were instructed to use every possible effort to secure an increased application of payment by results ; and the Shipyard Labour Department, established under the Admiralty in February 1917, conducted an active campaign on behalf of the system in the shipbuilding centres.

From this time onward, the process of introducing payment by results advanced rapidly, often attended by considerable workshop friction. In most cases, the question of piece-work versus time-work was, under the rules of the Trade Unions, one which fell within the discretion of each separate District Committee. The District Committees could either admit or reject payment by results, and could define, subject to a limited control by the Executive Councils of the Unions, the conditions under which it might be worked. In order that the system might be extended, it was therefore necessary for the Government either to persuade the various District Committees to accept it, or to override their veto. What was actually done varied from case to case. Some Unions, such as the shipwrights, agreed to the introduction of piece-work systems on a considerable scale ; others, such as the carpenters and patternmakers, remained altogether opposed. In the general engineering crafts there were big differences between district and district. In some areas the District Committees successfully stood out, right up to the end of the war, against the introduction of any form of payment by results ; but in the majority of areas, where piece-work had already some hold before the war, both it and the various bonus systems were applied more and more extensively, sometimes with the approval, but more often either with the reluctant consent, or in face of the opposition, more or less determined, of the Trade Union District Committees concerned.

Naturally, the brunt of the negotiations in most of the cases in which payment by results was being introduced, or in which the employer was attempting to introduce it, into a particular establishment, fell upon the shop stewards and Works and Workshop Committees. During 1917 and 1918 these were among the questions with which the workshop movement was principally concerned. The lines of dilution had already been worked out with sufficient clearness for most of the questions arising out of it to be fairly easily settled ; and, although in 1917 there were protracted disputes on the question whether dilution should be applied on private, or ' commercial ', as well as on munitions work, this was only a serious problem in most of the workshops for a few months. The handling of cases arising out of payment by results occupied an ever-increasing proportion of the time and energies of the shop stewards' movement, in so far as these were concentrated on essentially workshop problems.

The reason for this growing preoccupation lay, not solely in the fact that payment by results was being rapidly extended, but also in the fact that attempts were constantly being made to apply new, and often ' fancy ', systems of wage-payment. Before the war, although a few shops had introduced the ' premium bonus system ', usually the modified ' Rowan ' system originally devised upon the Clyde, there was, as a rule, very little variety in the systems of wage-payment adopted. The only frequent alternatives, in factory industries, to time-work were ' straight ' individual piece-work, and collective (or group or ' fellowship ') piece-work. But during the war an immense variety of fresh methods of payment was intro-duced. Factory after factory devised its own ' bonus ' system, either on an individual or on a collective basis, and experiments were made with all manner of scientific formulae of payment for ensuring the maximum output on each particular type of operation.

Here again was a group of questions which presented work, and a reason for activity, for the shop stewards. They had constantly to negotiate with the management when it was proposed that some new system of payment should be introduced ; and, as many of the workers often found it difficult to understand the basis on which their earnings were calculated, the stewards had also to deal with a steady stream of individual cases and complaints, the official district machinery of the Trade Unions being invoked only when serious difficulties arose.

Thus it will be seen that the growing prevalence of payment by results in the munitions industries meant increased activity on the part of the stewards, whatever the attitude of the workers towards it might be. If it was decided to insist on the retention of the time-work basis of payment, constant vigilance was required. If it was decided to acquiesce in the introduction of some form of payment by results, it was necessary both to lay down in consultation with the management the rules governing its operation, and to deal with all complaints and difficulties arising out of its actual working. During the later period of the war these questions, fully as much as the continued advance of dilution, afforded constant workshop preoccupations for the shop stewards, and caused them to retain their hold upon the mass of the workers.

CHAPTER VIII

SHOP STEWARDS AND ' RECOGNITION '

As we have seen, there was, before the war, no formal provision for the ' recognition ' of shop stewards by the employers. Nor, as long as the stewards confined themselves to the official duties prescribed for them in the Trade Union rule books, was there, as a rule, much room for recognition ; for the stewards possessed no negotiating functions, and their duties were confined to reporting to the District Committees, which would, in case of need, see that any question was taken up with the employers through the official Trade Union machinery. In the ' York Memorandum ', or ' Provisions for Avoiding Disputes ', signed by representatives of the Engineering Employers' Federation and the Amalgamated Society of Engineers on the 17th of April, 1914, the previously existing practice in respect of workshop negotiations was expressed in the following terms, and permitted to continue as the basis of negotiations pending the conclusion of a new agreement in place of that which had just been terminated on notice given by the A.S.E. :

> When a question arises, an endeavour shall be made by the management and the workmen directly concerned to settle the same in the works or at the place where the question has arisen. Failing settlement, deputations of workmen, who may be accompanied by their Organizing District Delegate (in which event a representative of the employers' association shall also be present), shall be received by the employers by appointment without unreasonable delay for the mutual discussion of any question in the settlement of which both parties are directly concerned. In the event of no settlement being arrived at, it shall be competent for either party to bring the question before a local conference to be held between the local association and the local representatives of the Society.

Although this agreement actually applied only to the A.S.E., the provisions were practically identical in the case of other Trade Unions. No mention was made of shop stewards and workshop organizations, which would indeed be largely ruled out as negotiating bodies by a strict interpretation of the words ' directly concerned '. Troubles, indeed, not seldom arose over this question ; and the precise degree of workshop recognition that was permissible was often in dispute. Particular firms, however, especially among those which were outside the Engineering Employers' Federation, frequently conceded a larger measure of recognition to shop stewards and formal or informal works committees, where these were in existence.

As soon as dilution began to be introduced we have seen that this involved workshop consultation on a far more considerable scale. At first this was allowed to develop informally, and some measure of recognition was granted by many ' federated ', as well as by ' unfederated ', firms. When the organized Dilution Scheme of the Ministry of Munitions was brought forward in the autumn of 1915, it became necessary to lay down more precise rules of procedure. The Central Labour Supply Committee, appointed as an advisory body to the Ministry of Munitions in September 1915, and consisting of Government representatives, employers, and Trade Unionists, was entrusted with the drafting of the Dilution Scheme. In addition to the important circulars L 2 and L 3, prescribing the rates of wages to be paid to men and women introduced under the scheme, the Committee drafted a number of other circulars, laying down the procedure to be adopted. The most important of these was Circular L 6, which defined the forms of consultation with the Trade Unions to be followed in carrying out the provisions of the Treasury Agreement and of Schedule II of the Munitions of War Act, 1915.[1]

In Schedule II, which embodied most of the provisions of the Treasury Agreement of March 1915, paragraph 7 contained the following provisions :

Due notice shall be given to the workmen concerned, wherever practicable, of any changes of working conditions which it is desired

[1] See Chapter VI, ante.

to introduce as a result of the establishment becoming a controlled establishment (i. e. controlled under the Munitions Act), and opportunity for local consultation with workmen or their representatives shall be given if desired.

Still, it will be noted, there is no mention of shop stewards or of workshop organization as such, and it is left quite open whether the ' consultation ' is to take place in the workshop or between the employer and the district Trade Union organization. The employers usually contended that the procedure to be followed was that of the ' York Memorandum ' quoted above.

Circular L 6 was an attempt to define and improve the procedure of ' consultation ' laid down in Schedule II. The principal clauses in it, bearing upon this point, are as follows :

The Minister (of Munitions) is of opinion that the following procedure should be adopted by a controlled establishment when any change is made in working conditions :

1. The workmen in the shop in which a change is to be made should be requested by the employer to appoint a deputation of their number, together with their local Trade Union representative if they desire, to whom particulars of the proposed change could be explained.

2. At the interview the employer, after explaining the change proposed and giving the date when it is to come into operation, should give the deputation full opportunity of raising any points they desire in connexion therewith, so that if possible the introduction may be made with the consent of all parties.

3. Should the deputation be unable at the interview to concur in the change, opportunity should be given for further local consultation, when representatives of the Trade Unions concerned might be present.

4. It is not intended that the introduction of the change should be delayed until concurrence of the workpeople is obtained. The change should be introduced after a reasonable time, and if the workpeople or their representatives desire to bring forward any questions relating thereto, they should follow the procedure laid down in Part I of the (Munitions of War) Act.

5. It is not desirable that formal announcement of the proposed change should be put on the notice board of the shop until intimation has been given as above to the men concerned, or their Trade Union representatives.

While this is so, the Minister is of opinion that it would be consistent with prudence that every endeavour should be made by employers to secure the co-operation of their workpeople in matters of this description.

Any difficulties experienced by either employers or workpeople should be at once referred to the Ministry, in order that an immediate endeavour may be made to find a satisfactory solution.

In the above circular, the recognition of workshop bargaining in connexion with dilution has become rather more distinct ; but there is still no explicit reference to shop stewards or shop committees, and the whole of the procedure is defined in essentially pre-war terms. The workpeople are to be asked to appoint a ' deputation ', and this ' deputation ' is the body with which the management is to discuss the proposal.

In fact, of course, the pre-war method of *ad hoc* deputations was already, at the end of 1915, falling into disuse, and being replaced by the method of continuous workshop organization. Even if the employer persisted in referring to the representatives whom he met as a ' deputation ', he very often knew well that he was really meeting the spokesmen of the Shop Stewards' Committee.

Circular L 6, which was issued in October 1915, was only a recommendation from the Ministry of Munitions to all firms desirous of introducing dilution, and had not behind it the same legal force as Schedule II of the Munitions of War Act. Consequently, many employers disregarded it, and a good deal of friction was caused by attempts to introduce dilution without workshop consultation. These, of course, played their part in calling out the energies, and increasing the appeal, of the workshop movement. Whether or not the employer consulted the workers, the effect was from this standpoint largely the same. Either consultation or failure to consult meant an increase in the activity of the new movement towards workshop organization.

The Trade Unions naturally preferred to secure the fullest consultation, and, from the end of 1915 onwards, their efforts were directed to making Circular L 6 compulsory on all employers who introduced any measure of dilution. The Ministry of Munitions, however, was throughout very remiss in enforcing on employers the procedure recommended, and refused altogether to give to it the force of law. Circular L 6, therefore, while it undoubtedly assisted the growth of the workshop movement, did not result, as it might have done, in the working out of a uniform procedure for all establishments, or in a general measure of recognition for the growing workshop organizations.

When the special Dilution Commissions for the Clyde and Tyne were appointed at the beginning of 1916, they set out, as we have seen,[1] to apply the general principles of the approved Dilution Scheme to each particular establishment in the areas under their control, by working out a special detailed scheme for each. Most of the workshop agreements or regulations in which these schemes were embodied contained definite provisions laying down the position as to workshop bargaining and workshop organizations in relation to them. For example, in one of the special schemes drawn up for a particular establishment, the following clauses are to be found :

> (3) A Shop Committee of the workers is to be formed to confer with the management on any point resulting from the practical operation of the Dilution Scheme which it has not been possible to settle between the individual worker concerned and his foreman. If, after the matter has been brought before the management by the Shop Committee and discussed, a mutual understanding is not arrived at, the matter in dispute shall, without stoppage of work, be referred to arbitration, in accordance with the provisions of the Munitions Acts.

> (b) No alteration shall take place in this scheme unless due notice is given to the workmen concerned and the procedure followed as presented by Clause 7 of Schedule II of the Munitions of War Act, 1915.

Most of the special Dilution Schemes from 1916 onwards included some clauses of this sort. The actual provisions differed from case to case. Sometimes, as above, the Committee established was a purely Trade Union body : in other cases it was a joint body, representing the management as well as the workers. Sometimes, instead of seeking to establish a new

---

[1] See Chapter VI, *ante.*

body, the Scheme merely recognized an already existing committee of shop stewards. Usually, skilled workers only were represented on the Committees or on the Trade Union side of joint committees ; for, the purpose being to safeguard the position of the skilled workers in face of dilution, it was often held that they alone were eligible or had the right to be consulted under the Munitions Act.

Whatever the actual form of organization might be, the general effect of the various schemes of dilution was to compel most employers to concede some sort of *de facto* recognition to the shop stewards and Workshop Committees set up in their works. The scope and limits of the recognition were undefined ; and serious disputes sometimes arose when the stewards claimed a responsibility or a right which a particular employer, or the employers as a body, refused to concede. Thus, on the 26th of November 1917, a serious strike broke out at Coventry, the point at issue being the measure of recognition to be conceded to shop stewards. The dispute was provisionally settled early in December, the Trade Unions and employers undertaking to deal with the whole question of ' recognition ' on a national basis, and to endeavour to draw up a national agreement defining the status and functions of shop stewards in all establishments throughout the engineering industry. National Conferences between the Trade Unions and the Employers' Federation in the engineering industry were held with this object in December 1917, with the result that the majority of the Trade Unions concerned signed a ' National Shop Stewards' Agreement ' jointly with the Engineering and National Employers' Federation. The largest Trade Union, however, the Amalgamated Society of Engineers, and one or two of the smaller Societies, refused to sign the agreement, on the ground that the measure of recognition accorded was inadequate. The members of these Societies, accordingly, continued through 1918 to appoint their stewards without any form of official recognition by the employers' associations. They represented, however, so large a proportion of the skilled workers in the industry that they were practically able to render inoperative the agreement entered into by the other Unions. In practice, nearly all employers granted recognition along the lines laid down in the abortive agreement; but the Unions were free from any obligation to respect the limitations on the activities of shop stewards which the employers had sought to impose. The boundaries of recognition remained undefined ; but the general tendency was towards a greater concession of it by the employers.

It was not until after the conclusion of the war that anything was done to clear up this indefinite situation. When, after the Armistice, negotiations for a post-war agreement were begun between the engineering employers and the Trade Unions, the question of the shop stewards' position was at once raised. The Amalgamated Society of Engineers agreed to accept temporarily the terms of the existing Shop Stewards' Agreement, on condition that a new one was immediately to be considered. The result was an amended agreement, which was accepted at a national joint conference on the 20th of May 1919. This agreement, which in theory at least determines the position of all recognized shop stewards and workshop organizations in the engineering and kindred industries throughout the country, has to be quoted in full.

SHOP STEWARDS

The following is a copy of the agreement in regard to the appointment and functions of shop stewards and works committees :

York, 20th May 1919.

REGULATIONS REGARDING THE APPOINTMENT AND FUNCTIONS OF SHOP STEWARDS AND WORKS COMMITTEES

With a view to amplifying the provisions for avoiding disputes by the recognition of shop stewards and the institution of works committees, it is agreed as follows :

(a) Appointment of Shop Stewards

1. Workers, members of the above-named Trade Unions, employed in a federated establishment may have representatives appointed from the members of the unions employed in the establishment to act on their behalf in accordance with the terms of this agreement.

2. The representatives shall be known as shop stewards.

3. The appointment of such shop stewards shall be determined by the Trade Unions concerned, and each Trade Union party to this agreement may have such shop stewards.

4. The names of the shop stewards and the shop or portion of a shop in which they are employed and the Trade Union to which they belong shall be intimated officially by the Trade Union concerned to the management on election.

(b) *Appointment of Works Committees*

5. A works committee may be set up in each establishment consisting of not more than seven representatives of the management and not more than seven shop stewards, who should be representative of the various classes of workpeople employed in the establishment.

The shop stewards for this purpose shall be nominated and elected by ballot by the workpeople, members of the Trade Union parties to this agreement, employed in the establishment.

The shop stewards elected to the works committee shall, subject to re-election, hold office for not more than twelve months.

6. If a question failing to be dealt with by the works committee in accordance with the procedure hereinafter laid down arises in a department which has not a shop steward on the works committee, the works committee may, as regards that question, co-opt a shop steward from the department concerned. An agenda of the points to be discussed by the works committee shall be issued at least three days before the date of the meeting if possible.

(c) *Functions and Procedure*

7. The functions of shop stewards and works committee, so far as they are concerned with the avoidance of disputes, shall be exercised in accordance with the following procedure :

(*a*) A worker or workers desiring to raise any question in which they are directly concerned shall in the first instance discuss the same with their foreman.

(*b*) Failing settlement, the questions shall be taken up with the shop manager and / or head shop foreman by the appropriate shop steward and one of the workers directly concerned.

(*c*) If no settlement is arrived at the question may, at the request of either party, be further considered at a meeting of the works committee. At this meeting the O.D.D.[1] may be present, in which event a representative of the Employers' Association shall also be present.

---

[1] O.D.D. = Organizing District Delegate, the full-time official of the Trade Union in the area.

(*d*) Any question arising which affects more than one branch of trade or more than one department of the works may be referred to the works committee.

(*e*) The question may thereafter be referred for further consideration in terms of the ' Provisions for Avoiding Disputes '.

(*f*) No stoppage of work shall take place until the question has been fully dealt with in accordance with this agreement and with the ' Provisions for Avoiding Disputes '.

(*d*) *General*

8. Shop stewards shall be subject to the control of the Trade Unions, and shall act in accordance with the rules and regulations of the Trade Unions and agreements with employers so far as these affect the relation between employed and workpeople.

9. In connexion with this agreement shop stewards shall be afforded facilities to deal with questions raised in the shop or portion of a shop in which they are employed. Shop stewards elected to the works committee shall be afforded similar facilities in connexion with their duties, and in the course of dealing with these questions they may, with the previous consent of the management (such consent not to be unreasonably withheld) visit any other shop or portion of a shop in the establishment. In all other respects shop stewards shall conform to the same working conditions as their fellow workers.

10. Negotiations under this agreement may be instituted either by the management or by the workers concerned.

11. Employers and shop stewards and works committees shall not be entitled to enter into any agreement inconsistent with agreements between the federation or local associations and the Trade Unions.

12. For the purpose of this agreement the expression ' establishment ' shall mean the whole establishment or sections thereof according to whether the management is unified or sub-divided.

13. Any question which may arise out of the operation of this agreement shall be brought before the Executive of the Trade Union concerned or the Federation as the case may be.

14. This agreement supersedes the agreement dated 20th December 1917, entitled ' Regulations regarding the Appointment and Functions of Shop Stewards ', made between the Engineering Employers' Federation and the Trade Unions.

Signed on behalf of—
The Engineering and the National Employers' Federations :
    HENRY LAWTON, Chairman.
    J. McKIE BRYCE, Secretary.

Signed on behalf of—
Amalgamated Society of Engineers :
    J. T. BROWNLIE, Chairman.
    H. ADAMSON, Secretary.

This agreement, although it was a considerable advance upon the agreement of 1917, by no means gave the Trade Unions all that they desired. The Works Committees, for example, for which it made provision, were small *joint* bodies, and not fully representative committees, consisting solely of stewards from each grade or department. No provision was made for shop committees, and no special powers were assigned to shop conveners, or to head stewards who were not elected to the Works Committee. Elections to the Works Committee were to be by ballot, and not, as in many actual cases, by virtue of office as shop convener. Moreover, a rigid and uniform system was prescribed, whereas, from the Trade Union point of view, there was a great deal to be said for the elasticity of system which existed before any definite national agreement was made. It was the employer, anxious to put a definite limit to the amount of recognition he was expected to concede, who was desirous that a uniform system should be adopted.

Nevertheless, the Shop Stewards' Agreement of 1919 did represent for the Trade Unions a big advance on the pre-war position, even if it failed to concede all that the workers in the shops had been able to gain under the abnormal conditions of the war period. The right to carry collective bargaining into the workshops, and to establish definitely Trade Union machinery in the shops themselves, was for the first time explicitly recognized, in such a way that it would be difficult for the employers, however circumstances might change, to take back what they had conceded. The shop stewards' organization lost, indeed, very greatly in power immediately on the termination of the war, when the shortage of labour which had been the basis of its strength ceased to exist. Many of the more active younger stewards were dismissed ; and the movement largely lost its militant character. But the gain represented by recognition was, as far as it went, a solid gain ; and the instrument of collective workshop bargaining which was created during the war years will undoubtedly be called again into play when a favourable occasion presents itself, and will remain permanently as an integral part of the machinery of Trade Unionism.

CHAPTER IX

SHOP STEWARDS—'OFFICIAL' AND 'UNOFFICIAL'

The account given in the preceding chapter of the progressive 'recognition' accorded to the shop steward system during the war period would be essentially incomplete if it were left at the point to which we have so far carried it. In an earlier chapter, attention was drawn to the existence, throughout the war period, to two types of shop stewards—'official' and 'unofficial'—the former definitely appointed and authorized to act by a Trade Union, and the latter appointed by a body of workers in a particular shop, without any form of Trade Union ratification. Stewards of the latter class were, however, more and more, as the war proceeded, authorized to act by the various unofficial 'Workers' Committees', of which an account has already been given.[1]

The Workers' Committees, and the 'left wing' of the shop stewards' movement as a whole, were throughout opposed to official 'recognition' by the Trade Unions, and to recognition by the employers in the form in which it was conceded under the Shop Stewards' Agreements of 1917 and 1919. They held the view that the official Trade Unions were under reactionary domination, and that the mission of the shop stewards' movement was to act as a militant organization within Trade Unionism, but in no sense responsible to the official leaders. If recognition by the employers was to involve, as it did under the Shop Stewards' Agreement, the subordination of the stewards to their respective Trade Unions, the Workers' Committees would have none of it.

A further reason for this attitude lay in the fact that practically all the Trade Unions were either 'craft' bodies, confined to tradesmen of a particular craft or group of crafts, or general labour bodies, organizing the less skilled workers apart from the skilled. The more advanced shop stewards were,

[1] See Chapter IV, *ante.*

as we have seen, ' Industrial Unionists,' who believed in the common organization of all workers, ' regardless of craft, grade, or degree of skill.' The Workers' Committee movement, as far as its powers went, had this ' industrial ' basis ; but, from the standpoint of its adherents, official recognition would mean the breaking into fragments of the ' industrial ' solidarity which had been unofficially secured, and an acceptance of the ' craft ' basis of the Trade Unions.

The question whether ' recognition of shop stewards ', either by the Trade Unions or by the employers, was or was not to be desired was hotly debated among Trade Unionists during the later years of the war period. The official Trade Union leaders, at first inclined to desire the granting of as little recognition as possible, gradually came, where they were far-seeing, to desire recognition in order to prevent the growth of a rival power not amenable to Trade Union discipline. On the other hand, many of those who were far from desiring recognition or officialization for its own sake, came to favour it because they doubted the power of the unofficial movement to continue in existence when the abnormal conditions of the war period were no longer present.

The question of recognition of the stewards by their Unions was, of course, largely fought out in the branches and delegate meetings of the Unions themselves. The attitude of the Workers' Committee leaders towards the official Trade Union District Committees varied from case to case. Sometimes the ' rank and file ' leaders stood for, and secured, the official positions on the bodies governing district Trade Union policy ; but in many cases there was a disposition to refuse to stand for office, in order that the unofficial character of the workshop organizations may be preserved intact. Consequently, the government of the Trade Unions, both nationally and locally, and the task of modifying their rules and practices so as to provide for the new situation caused by the emergence of the workshop movement, was left largely to the more moderate sections of the right and centre, with only a sprinkling of the extreme ' left wing ' elements.

We have seen how, after the Coventry dispute in 1917, the negotiations which resulted in the abortive Shop Stewards' Agreement of December 1917 were begun. We have seen, too, how a workable agreement was at last reached in May 1919. But, in addition to arranging for the recognition of shop stewards by the employers, the Trade Unions had the no less important task of assigning to the stewards, and to workshop organizations of all sorts, their due place in the structure of Trade Unionism. The first stages of this process of adjustment were carried through administratively. Under the rules of the Unions the proceedings of the various District Committees had to come regularly under review by the National Executives. As the various District Committees expanded and developed their regulations governing the appointment and duties of the shop stewards, these regulations came up for ratification, and gradually a body of precedents was created. The new situation was, however, found to strain very greatly the existing Trade Union rules dealing with the appointment and duties of shop stewards,[1] and it was speedily realized that these rules would need to be amended. In a piecemeal fashion this was done in a number of cases, and greatly enlarged powers for the stewards were laid down. In 1920, when a number of the principal Trade Unions concerned, including the Amalgamated Society of Engineers, were absorbed into a single body, the Amalgamated Engineering Union, advantage was taken of the change to codify, in the new rule book, the regulations governing the position of shop stewards and of workshop organization in relation to the wider government of the Trade Union movement. The new rules then adopted contained the following provisions on these points :

    (c) Rules of Amalgamated Engineering Union, as adopted in 1920.
        Rule 13, Clause 18 and Part of Clause 19, and Clause 6 of
        same rule.

    (18) District Committees shall authorize the appointment of Shop Stewards and Shop Committees in works and departments thereof in their respective districts, such stewards (who must have three years' full membership) and committees to be under the direction and control

---

[1] For quotations from these pre-war rules, see Chapter II, *ante.*

of the District Committee. Subject to national agreements, the powers and duties of Shop Stewards and Shop Committees shall be defined by the District Committees with the approval of the Executive Council. The Shop Stewards or the Shop Committee in a works or department thereof may appoint a convener, whose powers and duties shall be defined in like manner as the powers and duties of Shop Stewards and Shop Committees.

The powers and duties of Shop Stewards, Shop Committees, and conveners shall include the following :

(a) To examine periodically the contribution cards of all members, to use every endeavour to see that all men starting are duly qualified Trade Unionists, and that all persons are receiving the approved rates, and complying with the practice of the shop and district, and for these purposes to examine cards and pay-tickets, and to report to the District Committee any case in which the position is not satisfactory and cannot be adjusted within the shop.

(b) To report regularly, and at least once in every quarter, in writing to the District Committee on all matters in the shop affecting the trade, and to keep the District Committee posted with regard to all events occurring in the shop.

(c) To interview foremen or any other persons representing the management on any question arising in the shop or department provided that (a) no question involving a principle, change of practice, or stoppage of work shall be determined in any shop until it has been reported to and ratified by the District Committee, and (b) that in all matters Shop Stewards, conveners, and committees shall act within the rules and principles laid down by the District Committee and for the Executive Council, and in national or district agreements.

At least once in every quarter the District Committee shall convene a meeting of the shop stewards in the district. They shall be paid 4s. for each quarterly report : namely 3s. for duty performed, and 1s. for attendance and report to committee (conveners of Shop Stewards shall receive 6d. extra) ; these to be payable by the District Committee. If it is necessary for stewards to attend other meetings of the committee they shall be remunerated the same as witnesses attending committee meetings.

(19) District Committees shall also have power to call aggregate meetings, or shop meetings, upon trade questions.

(6) Shop Stewards shall be directly represented on the District Committee on the basis of one Shop Steward for every 10,000 members or part thereof.

The representative of the Shop Stewards on the District Committee shall be elected at a meeting of Shop Stewards, called by the District Secretary, in June and December.

Comparison between these rules, which were the direct consequence of the war-time developments, and those in force in 1914 will at once show the extent to which the importance of shop stewards and of workshop organization, as integral parts of the recognized machinery of Trade Unionism, increased during the war period. The appointment of both stewards and shop committees is no longer purely permissive, but is part of the regular duties of the District Committee. The appointment of a ' convener ' in each works or department is still permissive, but practically follows as a matter of course. The duties laid down for the stewards and committees are no longer confined to reporting on developments and organization in the shop to the District Committee, but include, under Clause (c), an important, though subordinate, function of workshop negotiation, which implies the recognition of workshop organization by the employers. Moreover, for the first time, the shop stewards secure a small measure of distinct representation on the Trade Union District Committees. This is doubtless in the nature of an experiment, and is the result of a compromise between those who desired the District Committees to consist mainly of workshop representatives, and those who advocate the continuance of the present system of branch representation. But it is clear that shop representation, once introduced, stands a good chance of being more liberally recognized in future revisions of the Trade Union rule books.

The official recognition of the shop stewards by the Trade Unions was already extending rapidly during the war, although it was not until later that the necessary changes were made to bring the Union rules into harmony with the actual developments of the war years. But, during the war, the increased official recognition accorded to the official stewards by no means settled the question of workshop organization as a whole. For, with varying degrees of strength from place to place and from time to time, there existed the wholly unofficial organization of the Workers' Committees competing with the official Trade Union bodies for the allegiance of the stewards.

A description of the position on the Clyde in 1916 will serve to indicate what was apt to occur where workshop organization was strong and the left-wing elements were combined in a vigorous Workers' Committee. At the Labour Party Conference in January 1917 a Special Committee, with Mr. Robert Smillie as the Chairman, was set up to investigate the Trade Union questions arising out of the deportation from the Clyde area, in March 1916, of a number of leading shop stewards, mostly active members of the Clyde Workers' Committee. These deportations took place as the result of the unofficial strike, described elsewhere, which began at Parkhead Forge as the result of a dispute concerning the measure of recognition to be accorded to the Convener of Shop Stewards, and spread to a number of other establishments in the Clyde area. The Labour Party's Special Committee, in describing the organization of the Clyde Workers' Committee,[1] show that it was aiming largely at substituting its authority for that of the various Trade Union District Committees, and at becoming the representative organization for all the workshops on the Clyde. The Commission examined a number of witnesses connected with the Clyde Workers' Committee, one of whom gave evidence as follows :

> . . . if you take the membership of the Clyde Workers' Committee, when the men in the workshop agreed to affiliate to the Clyde Workers' Committee, they usually sent their shop stewards as their representatives, so that as a matter of fact being a shop steward was one of the qualifications for being the representative on the Committee. Where they previously had sent their shop stewards to the Society to report to their District Committee, the shop stewards were sent to the Clyde Workers' Committee. . . . It was not absolutely necessary for your shop to send you ; you could represent a minority in the shop just the same as a majority, even though the minority was one.

Thus, in some shops all the stewards would be ' official ' stewards, and would report, and hold themselves responsible, to the various District Committees. In others, the shop meeting would go ' unofficial ', and would decide to repudiate the

[1] For further extracts from the Report, see Appendix C.

District Committees, and send its representatives only to the Workers' Committee. In yet others, the men would be divided, and the stewards would be partly official and partly unofficial. Nor was it by any means rare for a particular steward, or group of stewards, to double the posts, and to report both to the various District Committees and to the Workers' Committee. It was, in many cases, almost impossible to say whether a particular steward was official or unofficial; and this question in fact affected his position very little in day to day workshop negotiation. The unofficial stewards usually secured about the same degree of recognition from the management as the official stewards, except in some shops where, being in a minority, they were excluded from negotiation by the official stewards themselves.

But, whatever the position of the unofficial stewards might be in the workshops, the Workers' Committees remained throughout wholly unofficial and unrecognized. When, at the beginning of 1916, the Special Dilution Commission came to the Clyde for the purpose of installing the Government Dilution Scheme in the various establishments, they negotiated freely with the shop stewards, official and unofficial alike, whom they found actually exercising power in the shops. When, however, the Clyde Workers' Committee attempted, as a body, to open up negotiations with the Commissioners, the request was refused in the course of the following correspondence :

18th Feb. 1916.   THE GOVERNMENT COMMISSION ON
                              DILUTION OF LABOUR.

At a meeting of delegates representing twenty-nine Shops and Yards in the engineering Industry on the Clyde, met to consider the question of Dilution of Labour, I was instructed to enquire when it would be convenient for the Commissioners to receive a Deputation elected by that meeting to place the result of the Delegates' deliberations before the Commission.

I herewith conform with that request.

Hoping for a favourable reply,

Yours respectfully,

(Signed)   J. M. MESSER (Secretary, Clyde
                              Workers' Committee).

26th Feb. 1916.

Sir,

The Commission has now considered your letter of the 18th inst., receipt of which was acknowledged by the Secretary of the Commission on the 21st of February 1916, and desire that you should convey their thanks to your Committee for the proposal that delegates of the Clyde Workers' Committee should wait upon the Commission with reference to the dilution of labour.

The scheme of dilution of labour upon which this Commission is engaged, as you are doubtless aware, follows upon the agreement dated March 19th, 1915, between the various Trades Unions and the Government. Having regard to that Agreement, the Commissioners make it their practice to communicate with and consult the Trade Unions representing the particular trades affected by each particular scheme of dilution which the Commissioners from time to time consider, and, in addition, they consult the individual men affected by this scheme in the particular Shop concerned. As the Commissioners have found that the official Trade Unions in every case afford them full and sufficient assistance in reference to the details of each dilution scheme affecting their particular trades, and represent effectively their members, the Commissioners think it unnecessary to trouble your Committee in the matter, consisting, as they see it does, also of Trade Unionists.

I am, Sir,

Your obedient Servant,

LYNDEN MACASSEY,

per J. M. D.

It will be seen from this correspondence that the ground assigned by the Dilution Commissioners for their refusal to enter into relations with the Clyde Workers' Committee was that, as dilution was being introduced in consultation with the official Trade Union bodies, it would create an impossible situation if the Government also consented to negotiate with unofficial organizations which repudiated the authority of the Trade Unions. Nor is there any doubt that the Trade Union officials and Executives gave full support to this attitude, and insisted that the Government should make all arrangements through them as intermediaries on behalf of the men. Difficulties even arose on more than one occasion because the Trade Unions objected to the conclusion, by the Government or its representatives, of workshop agreements for dilution with organized bodies of shop stewards, even where, as in Woolwich Arsenal, those stewards already possessed a considerable degree of Trade Union recognition. The Trade Union officials and committees were at this stage fearful lest their influence might be undermined by the growth of the unofficial workshop movement, and were accordingly inclined to be suspicious of all fresh assertions of power or responsibility in the hands of the workshop organizations. As something like a rule of custom was established defining the new and enlarged sphere of workshop action, and its relation to wider Trade Union activities, this suspicion tended to diminish; but the official Trade Unions at all times set their faces strongly against the concession of any sort of recognition to the wholly unofficial Workers' Committees.

As we have seen, the Workers' Committees, on their side, did not desire recognition from the Trade Unions. Recognition by the Government would, on occasion, have been valuable to them, as it would have increased their prestige, and enabled them to strengthen their hold over the workshop movement. If they could have got the Clyde Dilution Commissioners to negotiate with them, their standing among the Clyde workers would obviously have been bettered. But their aim was to remain as unofficial ' ginger ' organizations, seeking both to keep the spirit of revolt alive despite the restrictions imposed by war-time legislation on official Trade Union activities and to promote, by their propaganda, the re-creation of the Trade Union movement on new and militant lines, with the object of a complete transformation of the industrial system. In order to understand their position more completely, we must now undertake a closer examination of the ideals and theories which lay behind the Workers' Committee movement.

CHAPTER X

THE AIMS OF THE WORKERS' COMMITTEES

The Workers' Committee movement has produced no official and authoritative exposition of its objects and policy ; but there is a considerable pamphlet literature, written by prominent members of the movement, which can be taken as indicating with sufficient clearness its general ideas and tendencies. In 1918 Mr. J. T. Murphy, at one time the leading spirit in the Sheffield Workers' Committee, and also active in the national ' rank and file ' movement, published a pamphlet entitled ' The Workers' Committee : an Outline of its Principles and Structure.' In 1919 Mr. W. Gallacher, a President of the Clyde Workers' Committee, published jointly with Mr. J. R. Campbell, a pamphlet, ' Direct Action ', in which again an account was given of the structure and objects of the Workers' Committee movement. These two pamphlets agree so closely in the general forms of organization and action which they propose that it is safe to take them as expressing, at least on the broader points of principle, the essential aims and methods of the unofficial workshop movement.

Mr. Murphy begins by explaining that the whole tendency of modern large-scale Trade Union organization is towards ' government by officials '. The Trade Union official, however, lives remote from the workshop atmosphere, and whatever his intentions may be, does not succeed in retaining or understanding the actual spirit and feelings of the men in the shops. In Mr. Murphy's view, policy ought to be determined, not by a handful of leaders or official Trade Union representatives, but by the actual will of the members. ' Real democratic practice ', he urges, ' demands that every member of an organization shall participate actively in the conduct of the business of the society. . . . The functions of an elected Committee, therefore, should be such that, instead of arriving at decisions for the rank and file, they would provide the means whereby full information relative to any question of policy should receive the attention and consideration of the rank and file, the results to be expressed by ballot.'

According to Mr. Murphy, this 'real democracy' is altogether excluded by the present methods of Trade Union organization and action. The ballot, for example, is often employed ; but it is not a real ballot, for only a minority of the members actually bothers to vote. This points to something wrong in the way in which the ballot is usually taken. This is done at Trade Union branch meetings ; and this fact leads Mr. Murphy to a considera- tion of the relative values of organization on a branch and on a workshop basis.

> A ballot is usually taken in the branches, and the meetings are always summoned meetings, so we will consider now the branch as a unit of the organization. It is usually composed of members who live in certain areas, irrespective of where they work, and irrespective of the turn on which they work.
> These are important factors, and account for a great deal of neglect. Men working together every day become familiar to each other and easily associate, because their interests are common. This makes common expression possible. They may live, however, in various districts, and belong to various branches. Fresh associa- tions have therefore to be formed, which at the best are but tem- porary, because only revived once a fortnight at the most, and there is no direct relationship between the branch group and the workshop group. The particular grievances of any workshop are thus fresh to a majority of the members of a branch. The persons concerned are unfamiliar persons, the jobs unfamiliar jobs, and the workshop remote ; hence the members do not feel a personal interest in the branch meetings as they would if that business was directly con- nected with their everyday experience. The consequence is bad attendance at branch meetings and little interest. We are driven, then, to the conclusion that there must be direct connexion between the workshop and the branch in order to obtain the maximum concentration on business. The workers in one workshop should therefore be members of one branch.

Mr. Murphy was at one time connected with the Guild Socialist movement, and it was perhaps from the Guild Socialists, who had always urged the superiority of the workshop over the branch as the basis of Trade Union organization, that Mr. Murphy learnt to formulate the above view. But, whatever the source may ultimately have been, the essential truth of the view that workshop organization produced a more vigorous response than the official branch organization of the Unions was, during the war years, being daily proved by experience. So far at least, the basis of the Workers' Committee movement was psychologically sound.

From this Mr. Murphy went on to point out that not only was the shop superior to the branch as a basis of organization, but also, in their Trade Union branches, the workers were sharply divided one from another, craft by craft and section by section. From the industrial point of view the branch was a disintegrating, and the workshop an integrating, influence. The branches kept each craft and section apart : workshop organization could be used to bind them all together in a common fellowship and solidarity.

It was therefore urged that each section of workers in each Union should appoint its stewards, and that the stewards should come together to form the Shop Committee. All the Shop Committees connected with a particular firm or establishment should appoint representatives to a Works or Plant Committee. For all the workers in each industry in a district a Local Industrial Committee should be appointed, and all the Industrial Committees should unite to form the Local Workers' Committee, on a basis which would include all the workers in the area. The Local Industrial Committees in turn would be federated into National Industrial Committees, and from the National Industrial Committees representatives would be appointed to the National Workers' Committee.

This structure was, of course, for the most part theoretical ; for the Workers' Committee movement, although it obtained a hold locally in some other industries, including mining, was for the most part confined to the metal, engineering, shipbuilding, and kindred industries. District Local Industrial Committees existed here and there ; but for the most part the various shop or works organizations were linked up directly with the Local Workers' Committee, while the National Workers' Committee was, in effect, a federation of the Local Workers' Committees. The leaders of the movement, however, regarded the degree of organization which they had achieved as merely a beginning, and the structure described above is that to which they looked forward. The proposals made by Messrs. Gallacher and Campbell, in their pamphlet mentioned above, are in all essentials the same as those of Mr. Murphy.

Throughout his pamphlet, Mr. Murphy never clearly faced the problem of the relationship of the organizations which he and his colleagues were seeking to create to the existing official Trade Union movement. This movement was, indeed, strongly criticized; but it was nowhere stated whether the new rank and file organizations were intended merely to overcome and supersede it, or whether it was somehow to be transformed so as to fit into the new structure which they sought to establish in power. Mr. Murphy held that ' where possible, it is desirable for shop stewards to be officially recognized ', and that, in their appointment, ' due regard should be given to the particular Union to which each worker belongs.' It therefore appears that he contemplated that, as was actually the case in most areas, the Workers' Committee stewards should act also on behalf of their various Unions, and the movement as a whole work officially within the Trade Union movement. Messrs. Gallacher and Campbell seem to pay less attention to working within the Trade Union movement, probably because they wrote at a later date, when the revolutionary aspects of the Workers' Committees had come more definitely to the front.

Both the Murphy and the Gallacher-Campbell pamphlets, representing broadly the English and Scottish Workers' Committee movements, confine themselves mainly to questions of method; but it is clear in both that the object aimed at is nothing less than a complete transformation of the industrial system. The Workers' Committees were always, in this sense, revolutionary bodies, aiming at the overthrow of the capitalist system in industry, and at playing their part in the substitution for capitalism of some form of ' workers' control '.

This object had already been prominent in the Trade Union amalgamation movement before the war, and had been popularized both by the Amalgamation Committees, which were subsequently absorbed into the shop stewards' movement, and by the propagandist bodies of Industrial Unionists and Guild Socialists. The desire for ' control ' was capable of finding expression in many different forms of extremeness or moderation, and there was nothing necessarily revolutionary, in any catastrophic sense, in the advocacy of workers' control in industry. It was, however, an idea mainly popular among the younger schools of Trade Unionists and Labour ' intellectuals ', and there were obvious reasons why it should manifest itself with peculiar force in the workshop movement. For, as the Guild Socialists had seen clearly even before the war, any movement by the workers towards democratic control in industry would have to be rooted in the workshops, and would largely depend for its growth on the capacity of the workers' organizations to assume workshop control over the operations of production.

The demand for workers' control in industry received an important stimulus during the first year of the war, when the first attempts were being made to reorganize the engineering industry so as to secure a higher production of munitions. During the early months of 1915 a number of Local Armaments Committees were created for this purpose in the principal engineering centres. In some cases these Committees consisted wholly of employers, acting under the Government with the aid of a separate Advisory Committee of Trade Unionists. But in other cases, as on the Clyde and Tyne, the Armaments Committees were joint bodies, consisting of employers and Trade Unionists, and entrusted with wide, if somewhat undefined, powers in organizing the production of munitions of war. At the same time, National Shell Factories were established, sometimes under the Armaments Committees, in a number of centres ; and the Trade Unions were in some cases given direct representation on the management of these factories.

During the summer and autumn of 1915 this representative

machinery created earlier in the year was gradually destroyed by the Government, and replaced by the bureaucratic machine of the Ministry of Munitions, which was established in June by a special Act of Parliament. Considerable friction accompanied the gradual scrapping of the Armaments Committee, especially in those centres, such as the Clyde and Tyne, in which the Trade Unionists had been most active in connexion with their work. Consequently, although the Government succeeded in superseding and disbanding them, a memory of this experiment in the representative organization of the munitions industry remained behind, and the brief experience of their work did a good deal to popularize the idea of workers' control.[1]

At Christmas time, in 1915, Mr. Lloyd George undertook a speaking tour on the Tyne and Clyde for the purpose of advancing the Government campaign for dilution. He had secured in the autumn the general approval of the official Trade Unions for the scheme prepared on the advice of the Central Munitions Labour Supply Committee; but considerable difficulties had already been experienced in its working, and the Trade Unions were pressing that the safeguards attached to the official scheme should be made legally enforceable. This was the main question at issue in connexion with the Munitions Amendment Bill, which was then before Parliament. The question of control had also been largely discussed in connexion with the acceptance of dilution by the Trade Unions, and a section of Trade Unionists had strongly urged that acceptance should be made conditional on the granting of a real measure of control over the administration of the Dilution Scheme to the organized workers.[2]

On the Clyde especially, Mr. Lloyd George had a warm reception. At his meetings he had to wrestle with the spokesmen

[1] For a further account of the Armaments Committee, see my *Labour in War-Time* and the *Labour Year Book* of 1916. See also the companion study, *Trade Unionism and Munitions*.

[2] See especially the pamphlet, *The Price of the Dilution of Labour*, written for the Amalgamated Society of Engineers by G. D. H. Cole and W. Mellor in November 1915.

of the Clyde Workers' Committee, who were up in arms against
the restrictions imposed on the Trade Unions by the Munitions of
War Act, and keenly critical of the arrangements for dilution
which were being made. It has been repeatedly asserted that
spokesmen of the shop stewards at these meetings told Mr. Lloyd
George that dilution would not be agreed to unless the workshops
were handed over to the sole control of the workers. Isolated
stewards may have made such statements in the heat of the
moment at the tumultuous meetings which Mr. Lloyd George
addressed ; but the Clyde Workers' Committee, as a body,
certainly made no such immediate claim. Its policy was
defined in the official organ, *The Worker*, on the 8th of January
1916, by Mr. J. W. Muir, who was at one time its secretary, in
the following terms :

> The Government must take over all the industries and national
> resources and give organized labour *a direct share in the management*
> down through all the departments.

In another part of the issue there is a report of Mr. Lloyd
George's meeting at Parkhead, in the course of which Mr. Kirkwood, one of the leaders who were deported from the Clyde
three months later, asked Mr. Lloyd George if he was prepared
to give the workers *a share in the management* of the works.[1]
It thus appears that the Clyde Workers' Committee was, at
this stage at least, demanding, not exclusive control, but only
a share in control on the lines which were urged in the official
A.S.E. pamphlet mentioned above. This demand followed
naturally upon the actual experience which they had had
during the months when the Local Armaments Committees
were being used by the Government as agencies for the organization of the munitions industries.

But, whatever the immediate claims put forward by the
leaders of the Clyde shop stewards may have been, there is no
doubt that, in a remoter sense, they were aiming at a complete
transformation of the industrial system, and at the substitution

[1] Both these passages are quoted in the Labour Party Special Committee's
Report, mentioned already, p. 17.

for the capitalist control of industry of a system based on communal control and involving full participation in management by the organized workers. This demand was indeed, even before the war, already coming to be part of the accepted policy of the more advanced sections of the Trade Union movement everywhere, and had been definitely included in the pre-war propaganda of the Metal, Engineering, and Shipbuilding Amalgamation Committee, and of its various local committees. The coming of dilution immediately caused this demand to assume a practical form, and the establishment of the Armaments Committees, the representation accorded to the Trade Unions in the management of certain of the National Factories, and the concessions secured by the shop stewards in certain works as the shortage of skilled labour became acute, all contributed to give precision to what was at first a vague and unformulated aspiration. Mr. Lloyd George need not have professed so much astonishment when the Clyde workers met him with the demand for control ; for the demand had been put forward, and fully discussed in the Labour press, for months before his visit.

At this time, however, the Government had set its face resolutely against the experiments in representative government of industry which had been made by a specially created department of the War Office before the Ministry of Munitions took over this part of its work. The whole attitude and tendency of the new ministry was bureaucratic. It was prepared to negotiate nationally, and to enter into national agreements, with the Trade Union leaders ; but it was opposed to the creation of local representative machinery, and intent on concentrating authority in the hands of divisional officers appointed from Whitehall and acting under Whitehall's instructions. The ultra-bureaucratic methods of the Employment Department of the Board of Trade, from which the leading officials on the Labour side of the new Ministry came, were adopted throughout all departments of its work, with the result that the advocates of representative organization, including those sections of the workers who were identified with the demand for a share in control, found themselves from the first in sharp opposition to the Ministry.

It must, however, be made plain that this opposition was, in the case of the ' left-wing ' shop stewards, far less opposition to dilution itself than to the methods of administration which found favour with the Ministry of Munitions. At the Parkhead meeting referred to above, Mr. Kirkwood, expressing the view often expressed in the declarations of the Clyde Workers' Committee, stated that

> We as Socialists welcome dilution of labour, which we regard as the natural development in industrial conditions. We are not like the Luddites of another generation who smashed the new machinery. But this scheme of dilution must be carried out under the control of the workers. We recognize that, if we have not the control, cheap labour will be introduced ; and, unless our demand is granted, we will fight the scheme to the death.[1]

There were, indeed, two opposite views about dilution in the ranks of the Labour movement itself. The older craftsmen who were less affected by Socialist ideas were opposed to it on the ground that it threatened the integrity and status of their crafts, and was likely to menace them with unemployment after the war. This was the conservative objection, and was at times very powerful. But the more advanced sections, especially on the Clyde, took up the view that dilution was a necessary stage in the evolution of machine industry, and that, although the very great speeding up of the process owing to the war had its dangers and demanded special measures for the protection of the workers, attention should be given, not to combating dilution, but to controlling it. Hence the added impetus given to the movement for ' workers' control ', and hence the keenness on organizing in Trade Unions the male and female dilutees, and on making them an integral part of the workshop organizations, which was far more marked among the left-wing shop stewards than among the more old-fashioned and steady-going Trade Unionists and Trade Union leaders.

Among the whole body of stewards, both these differing

[1] Quoted in the Labour Party Special Committee's Report, p. 17.

points of view, and also many intermediate varieties, were of course represented. The out-and-out opposition to dilution of the older craftsmen was often modified by the Socialist spirit of the younger men, while their demand for ' control ' was often blunted because it was a matter in which many of the older men took little interest. On the whole, the definitely ' left-wing ' elements were strongest on the Clyde ; and this may be why, although there were many disputes, dilution was perhaps pushed farther, and with less direct opposition, there than in any other important centre. It is quite a mistake to suppose that the ' out-and-out ' opposition to dilution came mainly from the extreme ' left '. This is disproved by the ease with which, on making concessions to the stewards in the matter of control, the Clyde Dilution Commissioners were able to secure practically any measure of dilution they wanted, subject to reasonable safeguards, in their various workshop schemes. It was in those shops in which traditions of highly skilled work were most strongly entrenched and highly valued, and were not counterbalanced by ideas about the ' materialistic ' evolution of industry, that the strongest absolute resistance to dilution was encountered.

The ' left-wing ' leaders were largely Marxians. They believed in the ' materialist conception of history ', and held that the blurring and elimination of craft distinctions represented a necessary stage in the overthrow of capitalism. Of course, many of those who followed their leadership had no such clearly defined theory in their minds ; but there is no doubt that the Marxian theory, side by side with ideas of industrial self-government which had been popularized by the Syndicalists and Guild Socialists in the years before the war, played a leading part in the development of the Workers' Committee movement.

In this chapter I have attempted to outline the industrial ideas which lay behind the Workers' Committees. But to leave the matter here would be to give an essentially incomplete account of their character, especially in the later phases of their development. For, although they began mainly as industrial bodies, seeking to meet an immediate situation which had arisen in the workshops, they became more and more, as the war continued, also political, both in these aims and in their day-to-day activities. It is necessary that we should now examine them from this point of view, and seek to estimate their importance as forces in the political sphere.

CHAPTER XI

POLITICS IN THE WORKSHOP MOVEMENT

FROM August 1914 to March 1916, Great Britain waged war under the voluntary system of military service. On the 27th of January 1916, despite the opposition of a fully representative Labour Conference, conscription was applied to single men under the first Military Service Act, which came into actual operation on the 2nd of March. Married men were brought within the scope of conscription by the second Act, passed on the 25th of May. A number of subsequent Acts of 1917 and 1918 increased the stringency with which military conscription was applied, and raised the age limit for exemption.

Munition workers were at first but little affected by the coming of conscription, for the need for a continual increase in the output of munitions was held to make their retention in the workshops indispensable. Already, under the voluntary system, it had been necessary to prevent the enlistment in the army of men engaged on vital industrial work, and this protection was maintained after the introduction of compulsory service. But gradually, as the demands of the army for men imposed an increasing strain upon the 'man-power' of the nation, the Government turned its eyes to the munition factories. Dilution was by this time firmly established, and was being rapidly extended. Accordingly, it was possible to a large extent to replace the less skilled munition workers who were eligible for military service either by women or by men who, for reasons of age or health, were ineligible. The process of 'combing out' the munition factories, therefore, began in earnest.

During 1916 the 'combing out' was almost wholly confined to the less skilled workers, although there were numerous cases in which disputes arose out of attempts of the military authorities to enrol skilled men. From November 1916 to

April 1917 the Trade Unions representing skilled workers were able, under an arrangement entered into with the Government, to issue to their skilled members ' trade cards ' of exemption from military service. But in April 1917 the Government suddenly terminated the ' trade card ' scheme, and brought all exemptions on trade grounds under direct departmental control. From this time onwards, constant recruitment of skilled workers took place on a large scale, the gaps in industry being filled by further rapid extension of dilution.[1]

From the standpoint of this study of the workshop movement during the war, these facts about military service are of fundamental importance, because they affected to a considerable extent the character and activities of the workshop organizations. The official Trade Unions, especially those which represented the skilled workers, found themselves turning more and more into agencies for securing the exemption of their members from military service. During 1917 and 1918 there was continual warfare between the Trade Unions and the National Service Department concerning both the principles governing the taking of men for the army, and the constant doubtful cases of individuals which arose. Trade Union officials spent a great part of their time negotiating over these questions, which also largely occupied the attention of the mass of the exempted workers.

Naturally, the workshop movement was also profoundly affected. Although the Government, in this case as well as in that of dilution, recognized only the official Trade Union bodies, and would have no dealings with the unofficial Workers' Committees, the latter, and the shop stewards of both kinds, were inevitably engaged largely in dealing with workshop questions of military service. By 1917, at any rate, most of the men who desired to enlist had done so, and reluctance to leave the shops for the army was therefore to be expected from many of those who remained. Moreover, the ceaseless bargain-

---

[1] For fuller details about the Military Service Acts in relation to industry, see *The Labour Year Book*, 1919, pp. 124–47, and the companion study, *Trade Unionism and Munitions*.

ing over exemptions tended to create a state of mind addition-
ally hostile to enlistment and to the causes which made necessary the ' combing out ' of the workshops. The tide of workshop
opinion had hitherto been flowing generally in favour of the
war, although there was from the first a considerable body of
international Socialists opposed to it. But, from the moment
when conscription seriously touched the workshops, the tide of
opinion began to set the other way, and the ' anti-war ' party
in the Trade Unions, and still more in the unofficial workshop
organizations, began rapidly to grow.

In March 1917 took place the first Russian Revolution,
which was heralded by the workers in all countries as a fore-
taste of the coming triumph of the Labour cause. Disillusion-
ment with its results, indeed, set in during the summer months ;
but its immediate effect was to give a huge stimulus to all
forms of ' left-wing ' organization, and to set the minds of the
younger groups in the Labour movement running in the direction of ' revolution '. The much-advertised unofficial ' Leeds
Conference ' of the 3rd of June 1917, called for the purpose of
forming Workers' and Soldiers' Councils, on the model of the
Russian Soviets, in Great Britain, was indeed abortive ; but,
although the Labour movement as a whole was far from being
converted to a revolutionary point of view, the revolutionary
tendencies in it were undoubtedly strengthened.

In November 1917 the second, or Bolshevik, Revolution in
Russia resulted in the definite assumption of power by the
Communists, who had secured a majority on the Soviets in the
big centres. The November Revolution sharply divided Labour
and Socialist opinion in every country in the world, and the
full results of the division have not yet, in many cases, become
manifest. In Great Britain they have been slow in showing
themselves in the national organization of the Trade Unions or
of the Labour Party, but they very rapidly made their impression upon the movement in the workshops. The ' left wing '
found itself, for the first time, equipped not only with a
theory, but also with an example, and this affected its whole
attitude, the character of its propaganda, and its relations to

the official Trade Union movement.   Long before there was a
definite Communist Party in Great Britain, the Bolshevik
Revolution had shown its influence in the development of the
workshop movement.

During the last two years of the war, then, the movement
in the workshops, without abandoning its industrial activities,
was assuming more and more a political complexion.   The tide
of opinion, still doubtless minority opinion, was beginning to
turn against the war policy of the Government and even against
the war itself.   There were other causes, such as high prices
and ' war weariness ', besides the extension of military service
and the revolutions in Russia, which contributed to this result ;
but these latter were particularly powerful factors in producing
a change of attitude in the workshops.   Dilution had been
primarily an industrial question—merely the intensification of
a process of industrial evolution which was developing more
slowly before the war.   The activities for which it called were
specifically industrial, and their effect was to concentrate the
attention of the workshop leaders upon purely industrial
problems.   But military service, while it produced powerful
reactions on industry, was clearly a political problem, and the
reflections and forms of action which opposition to recruitment suggested were necessarily political, and might easily
become revolutionary.

The revolutions in Russia, and especially the November
Revolution, seemed to many shop stewards obviously to point
the moral which had already been forming itself in their minds.
Russia had been in the war and had suffered hideous losses ;
Russia was now virtually—and soon absolutely—out of the
war because there the ' class conscious ' workers had seized
power and insisted upon peace.   Would not the workers in
other countries, and even in Great Britain, find in the adoption
of the same method the only way out of their own war-made
tribulations ?   The opposition of the Allied Governments to the
Soviet power, and the purposeless wars waged in the four corners
of Russia, deepened the suspicions in the workshops that a
Power so disliked by the ' capitalist Governments ' of Western

Europe must have found the way of emancipation for the working people.

It is no part of my purpose in this monograph to discuss these views. I am concerned only with their undoubted effect upon the spirit and attitude of the workshop movement. Gradually they converted the Workers' Committees from mainly industrial bodies aiming at a re-fashioning of the Trade Union movement on a more up-to-date basis corresponding to the integration of modern capitalism into nuclei of revolutionary organization, whose leaders regarded their industrial functions as important only in so far as they served to arouse discontent and ministered to the growth of the revolutionary spirit in the workshops.

This is not to say that the leaders of the Workers' Committees for the most part either greatly modified or greatly developed their theories. In the theoretical sense, they had been throughout revolutionaries, looking forward to the overthrow of capitalism by the mass power of the workers' organizations, and the growth of class consciousness among them. But the Bolshevik Revolution, and the unrest engendered by the long continuance of the war, transformed their revolutionism from a theory into a possible basis of action, and they began to imagine that, even in their time, their dreams might come true. From theoretical revolutionists they tended to develop into practical revolutionaries.

This is not to say that even the most extreme workshop leaders at any time set out to stir up an actual revolutionary outbreak in Great Britain. They knew well this was out of their power, and they told themselves that this is not how revolutions are made. The way in which the change of attitude made itself manifest was more subtle. It meant that actual workshop unrest, arising out of disputes over dilution, over military service, over the increasingly severe workshop discipline, approaching ' industrial conscription ', which compulsory service made possible, or over any other question, was differently regarded ; that strikes were more definitely regarded as means to the stimulation of ' class consciousness ', and that big, nation-wide manifestations of unrest were estimated with reference to the likelihood of their taking a positively revolutionary direction. The unofficial workshop movement became more and more the movement of a revolutionary minority seeking to act upon the ' apathetic mass ', and to draw it, by all available inducements, towards a more revolutionary outlook and policy.

Inevitably, the effect of this tendency was to widen the rift between the official and unofficial sections of the shop stewards' movement. Although official Trade Union opinion was passing through an evolution in some respects similar to that which was taking place in the workshops, it never became, in the common sense of the word, revolutionary, and it saw, in the later developments of the unofficial movement, more and more a menace to the maintenance of Trade Union organization as it was understood by the established leaders. This was certainly one of the motives which led to the wider measure of official recognition accorded by the Trade Unions to their official shop stewards during the later years of the war, and to the conclusion of the agreement with the employers in 1917 and 1919, under which official stewards were recognized by the latter also, and their functions as workshop negotiators defined. The idea was that, as the shop steward system had obviously come to stay, the best course was to regularize it, and so undermine the influence exercised by the ' unofficial ' movement even over many of the ' official ' shop stewards. The sense that this was the object of ' recognition ' also goes far to account for the hostile attitude adopted towards ' officialization ' by the Workers' Committee movement.

I fear lest what I have said above may be taken as implying a more definite and clearly marked change of attitude than actually took place at any stage. In fact, the whole development was gradual, and was by no means completed until after the end of the war, when the actual change in workshop conditions had effectually robbed the shop stewards and Workers' Committees of many of their war-time industrial functions. It is rather of a gradual shifting of emphasis than of a positive change of attitude that I am seeking to convey the impression. The workshop organizations did not drop their industrial activities : they carried them on right up to the conclusion of the war. But circumstances tended to subordinate the more purely industrial activities of the leaders in the shops to activities which were at least in part political, and the change of attitude caused by the Russian Revolution caused both a more ready acceptance, and an intensification, of the change of emphasis and the diversion of energy which were to some extent inevitable.

These changes, it has often been stated by shop stewards and leaders who were not in sympathy with the new developments, resulted in a change in the type of men who were selected and were ready to assume office as stewards. Among those who, like the Guild Socialists, attached importance to the workshop movement largely as a means to the development by the workers of an effective control over the management and conditions of the shops, it was often urged that the shop stewards' movement, in allowing itself to become preoccupied mainly with political issues, was neglecting the favourable opportunities presented by war-time workshop conditions of establishing effective ' workshop control ' under Trade Union auspices, and thus laying the foundations for a fundamental transformation of the industrial system.

It is difficult to estimate, in any quantitative sense, the force of the criticism ; but it is certain that in some areas, as on the Clyde, antagonism did develop between those stewards who regarded their principal mission in the workshops as one of revolutionary agitation and preparation for a coming day of struggle, and those who desired to concentrate, as far as possible, on the attempt to secure a real measure of workshop control. The latter group got the worst of this conflict. It was always a small minority, and it had not, in the same measure as the active minority upon the Workers' Committees, the power of acting upon the mass, and carrying the mass along with it. Perhaps this was in part because the policy of an ' encroaching ' conquest of workshop control made far more exacting and continuous demands upon the vigilance and mental activity of the workers than the rival policies ; but it was also largely because the purely industrial demand failed to respond to the largely political feelings of unrest which were becoming more and more pronounced as the war dragged on.

Thus, during the latter part of 1917, and during 1918, we find the various bodies of shop stewards, and especially the unofficial Workers' Committees, less and less swayed by the argument that industrial strife in time of war must be put aside, and more and more often issuing political declarations in favour of ' peace by negotiation ', participation in the projected Stockholm International Labour Conference, and so on. More and more, the ending of the war became a definite object, and stiffer and stiffer was the resistance encountered as the growing demands of the war involved ever more dilution, more withdrawals of men for military service, more rigid control over the free movement of workers from factory to factory.   And in the making of this change of attitude and emphasis, the most important factors were the extension of military service on a compulsory basis and the contagious influence of the Russian Revolution.

CHAPTER XII

MOVEMENTS ANALOGOUS TO THE WORKSHOP MOVEMENT

By far the greatest part of this monograph deals directly with the munitions industries, in which the most important developments of the workshop movement took place during the war period. But, at the same time, analogous movements were proceeding in other industries, although they attracted nothing like the same degree of public attention, and were nowhere on quite so considerable a scale.

In the first place, various attempts were made by Trade Unions or groups of workers in other industries to acclimatize and develop the shop steward system. Those industries which, like the printing and building industries, to a considerable extent possessed the system before the war, developed it considerably, and extended it to those crafts and classes of workers among which it had not previously existed on any considerable scale. Especially among the woodworkers did the system, spreading from the men engaged on army hut building and aircraft work, and from the shipyards, become general and powerful, and develop the same conflicts between 'official' and 'unofficial' movements as we have seen already in the munitions industries. The vehicle builders also adopted the system directly from the engineering trades, and from the railway locomotive shops it spread rapidly to other branches of railway work to which it was readily adaptable. Similarly, it spread from the engineering and kindred branches of the postal service to other departments of the Civil Service.

Attempts were also made to apply the system to other industries, or branches of industry, in which it had previously either not existed at all, or been very weak. The boot and shoe operatives, among whom a great deal of dilution and substitution of women's for men's labour took place in consequence of the huge demands of the Allied Armies, developed the system, particularly in such centres as Northampton, Kettering, and Wellingborough. In this case, however, probably because of the more highly standardized character of the industry, it developed no power at all corresponding to that which it was able to exercise in the engineering industry. The older Trade Union officials, under whose auspices the methods of collective bargaining and arbitration had been pushed very far before the war, were inclined to be suspicious of the new development; and, although many of the District Committees and officials favoured it, it did not make very rapid headway. There can be no doubt, however, that it has come to stay, and a measure of recognition has now been accorded to it under the Trade Union rules.

Another case in which repeated attempts were made to apply the system was the cotton industry of Lancashire and Cheshire. Here again, processes are very highly standardized, and collective bargaining has been carried very far, always under the auspices of the highly trained permanent Trade Union officials. Dilution took place in the cotton industry during the war, and women were introduced into certain branches, such as spinning, from which they had previously been almost wholly excluded. But the industry as a whole was, even before the war, largely a women's industry, and substitution largely took the form of a return of married women to their trades to take the place of men who were called up. Moreover, except in certain special branches, the volume of production was greatly contracted, and dilution on the scale practised in the munitions industries was, therefore, not required.

Nevertheless, an impetus was given to the movement for workshop organization, and, in a number of areas, attempts were made both by the spinning and by the manufacturing trades to install the shop steward system. Sometimes these attempts were made officially by the local association of spinners or weavers : in other cases, they arose unofficially among bodies of workers in the shops. The unofficial movements seem however, to have possessed for the most part little stability, and hardly any evidence is obtainable as to the actual working of bodies of either type. The system has, indeed, become firmly, and it would appear permanently, established among certain sections, and particularly in certain of the ' provinces ' of the Operative Spinners' Amalgamation ; but the functions of the stewards seem to be almost restricted, except when actual strikes arise, to the reporting of cases to the local officials. Among the weavers and other manufacturing trades, no stability of workshop organization seems to have been realized.

The movement of events in the woollen and worsted trades has been to some extent similar, but in this case the degree of Trade Union organization and collective bargaining reached before the war was far less, and the demands made upon the industry during the war greater and productive of greater changes. The attempts to apply the shop steward system, already partly in operation in the dyeing sections of the industry, were accordingly more numerous, but not much stability of organization has been secured. It has been clearly shown that the textile industries, with their more standardized methods of operation, and the essentially routine character of their work-shop processes, offer a less easy opening for the growth of workshop organization than the far more diversified engineering and kindred industries. It has been said that in a textile establishment nothing fresh ever happens, whereas, in an engineering shop there is something fresh every week ; and this difference goes far to account for the much bigger growth of workshop organization in the latter than in the former case.

Far more important than the direct attempts to apply the shop steward system in other factory industries are the largely analogous developments which took place during the war in industries which are not carried on under factory conditions. These occurred particularly in the coal mines and upon the railways.

We have seen already [1] that the mining industry is one in

<hr />

[1] In Chapter II.

which the material conditions themselves have resulted in a great measure of coincidence between Trade Union branch organization and the unit of the ' plant ' upon which the workers are employed.   Among the coal miners, the normal practice is for the Trade Union lodge to consist of all the Union members employed in a particular pit, or perhaps in a group of small pits.   Mining is a village industry, in which most of the men live near the scene of their work.   Pit meetings are therefore far easier to convene, and arise far more naturally, than among workers who live in a town, scattered among workers belonging to other occupations, and often at a considerable distance from their place of work.   Moreover, the fact that mining is a dangerous occupation results in a feeling of comradeship among the men working in a particular pit, and leads naturally to common action on the basis of the pit, especially where any question of safety is at issue.   The pit, which commonly coincides with the Union lodge, is therefore, in any case, the natural centre of mining Trade Union activity.   The lodge does not, indeed, normally include all the workers in the pit ; for certain special grades, such as the deputies and the enginemen, have usually their separate Trade Unions, which may, or may not, be affiliated to the Miners' Federation of Great Britain.   But these are only a very small proportion of the employees, and their separate organization does not very greatly affect the importance of the pit lodge as the unit of feeling and industrial activity.

In addition, a special feature of mining organization contributes very greatly to the importance of the pit as a unit. Under the law, the miners in any pit are entitled, if they so decide, to appoint an official of their own, a ' checkweighman ', whose official duty is to check the weights of coal brought to the surface on account of the various hewers.   The checkweighman, in practice, usually exercises far wider functions, and often becomes in fact a sort of full-time chief shop steward for the pit as a whole.   He undertakes a good deal of negotiation with the management over grievances and complaints arising in the pits, only calling in the Trade Union official, the district miners' agent, when he cannot get the question at issue settled directly with the aid of the Lodge Committee.

The ' checkweighing ' laws, designed to prevent fraud in the payment of miners' piece-work wages, have thus resulted in equipping the organized miners with a full-time works official at practically every pit ; for the permissive power to appoint a checkweighman is used wherever organization is strong. This helps very greatly both in maintaining the stability of pit organization and in keeping up close and regular contact with the district miners' associations. The readiness with which fully attended pit meetings can be summoned renders mining Trade Unionism essentially democratic at its base, and prevents the absorption of undue power by an official caste.

The actual structure of mining Trade Unionism underwent little alteration during the war ; for it was already well adapted to meeting the new situation which the war caused. The voluntary enlistment of mine-workers during the early part of the war was abnormally heavy, and before long it was necessary to prohibit the recruitment of miners except for the extraordinarily dangerous work of the tunnelling sections. Not until 1918 was the industry called upon to make further numerically important contributions from its man-power to the fighting forces ; and meanwhile it had been necessary to fill up the vacancies caused by enlistment with men drawn from other occupations.

As a result of enlistment, and also of the working out of seams and the restriction of fresh development work, the output of coal fell sharply, and the Government found it necessary to take special measures for its improvement. In February 1915 the Coal Mining Organization Committee, which included representatives of the miners and mine-owners, was set up, and this body acted on behalf of the Government in the stimulation of increased output until the beginning of 1917, when the whole of the mines were brought under State control, and a Coal Controller was appointed. The Coal Mines Organization Committee was then replaced by an Advisory Committee of miners and mine-owners, from which the miners subsequently withdrew on the ground that no notice was taken of their representations by the Government.

During 1916 the Government drew the attention of the miners and mine-owners to the necessity of reducing the amount of ' absenteeism ' in the industry, and of taking measures to secure a fuller week's work from every miner. Attempts were also made to get the Miners' Federation to agree to the suspension of the Coal Mines Eight Hours Act ; but to this the miners absolutely refused to consent. The Coal Mining Organization Committee was thereupon requested to take up the question of ' absenteeism ', and the Miners' Federation issued to its members more than one manifesto calling for more regular work. Throughout the industry, the actual average number of shifts worked during the week averaged slightly less than five before the war, the arduous nature of the work, of course, making continuous application to it more difficult than in most other industries. The action taken by the Miners' Federation resulted in a reduction of absenteeism, and a slight increase in the average number of shifts worked. But the Government was not satisfied that enough had been done ; and, in the autumn of 1916, proposals were made for the institution of a system of fines for absenteeism. The scheme, as it was finally worked out, provided for the setting up, at each colliery, of a Pit Committee, with the object of stimulating increased output, and with the power, similar to that possessed by the Munitions Tribunals established under the Munitions of War Acts, to fine absentees.

The miners at once raised the question of the amount of power which these proposed tribunals were to possess, and of the scope of their duties and functions. Absenteeism, it was pointed out, was by no means the only cause of low output, which might result just as much from the actions or attitude of the management as from those of the men. The miners therefore demanded that it should be possible to arraign colliery officials, as well as miners, before the tribunals, and to raise any question arising out of the management of the pit that might affect the output of coal.

Finally, a scheme was devised under which fairly elastic powers were secured by the Pit Committees. Officials as well as miners could be dealt with; and the limits of the Committees' power to deal with questions of management was left largely undefined. The scheme, in this form, was accepted by a Delegate Conference of the Miners' Federation in December 1916.

Pit Committees then began to be set up in the various coalfields. The system was never universally adopted, and in a number of areas friction speedily arose. The colliery owners persisted in regarding the new machinery as created purely for the purpose of dealing with absenteeism, and attempts to raise issues which involved the question of management were keenly resented. Disputes of this sort took place particularly in Notts. and Derbyshire and in South Wales; and in many areas the coal-owners or the management seem to have deliberately killed the Committees when they found that their activities could not be restricted to the question of absenteeism. This they were able to do, because the Committees, being joint bodies representing the management as well as the men, could not function without the co-operation of both parties.

The experiments in pit organization made under Government auspices therefore produced no considerable result; but it seems to be agreed that their institution, and even more their future, gave a stimulus to rank and file organization among the miners themselves. From time to time before the war, various forms of unofficial organization had sprung up in the mining industry. In various counties, such as Durham, there existed 'Miners' Forward Movements', which aimed, by rank and file action, at stimulating a more advanced policy within the official miners' associations. The South Wales Miners' Unofficial Reform Committee, which was responsible, in 1912, for the issue of that much discussed pamphlet, 'The Miners' Next Step', was the best known of these pre-war bodies.

The effect of the changes resulting from the war was, especially in 1917 and 1918, to promote fresh movements among the rank and file of the miners' associations, based

directly upon the natural ' workshop ' organization of the pit.
' Reform ' movements sprang up in Lancashire and Cheshire,
the Midlands, Durham, Scotland and Yorkshire, and, where the
coalfield was near any important munitions area, as in the
west of Scotland and South Yorkshire, the Miners' Reform
Committees entered into relations with the shop stewards'
movement and with the Workers' Committees in the towns.
The Lanarkshire Miners' Reform Movement, one of the most
vigorous, was in close relationship, in 1918, to the Clyde
Workers' Committee, and the South Yorkshire miners, in the
same year, sympathetically joined in some number in a munitions strike originating in Sheffield under the auspices of the
Workers' Committee. Fresh forms of organization were hardly
required for the growth of this rank and file movement. The
pit was already a natural ' workshop ' unit, and all that was
needed was that a pit meeting should elect its delegate or
delegates to the Reform Committee. As we shall see later,
this unofficial organization among the miners has continued
to grow since the end of the war.

On the railways the position was less simple than in the
case of the mines. The National Union of Railwaymen and the
other railway Trade Unions are highly centralized bodies, in
which almost all power is vested in the hands of the national
officials, national executives, and national delegate meetings.
District Councils, corresponding structurally to the District
Committees of such Unions as the engineers, exist ; but their
functions are widely different. They are excluded under the
rules from all share in the determination of policy or in the
administrative work of the Unions, and are supposed, at least
in the case of the N.U.R., to confine themselves to the task of
organization and propaganda. These restrictions resulted in
practice, and to an increased extent during the war, in the
assumption by the District Councils, in addition to their
officially recognized functions as propagandist bodies, of
unofficial functions, by the exercise of which they sought to
mould the official policy of the railway organizations. The
District Councils of the N.U.R. consist of delegates from the

various Union branches, and thus have not a ' workshop ' basis. But, except in the large towns, there is usually only one station and one branch, so that works organization and branch organization often tend to coincide. Even in the large towns, where there are a number of stations and branches, a particular branch often centres round a particular place of work. Moreover, the conditions of comparatively free mobility under which work is carried on tend to make each yard or station to some extent a natural centre of discussion, and thus to create an informal type of workshop organization. Thus, although the District Councils have no definite workshop basis, their methods of operation have, and had during the war, a good deal in common with those of the shop stewards' movement in other industries. In the railway locomotive shops, of course, the shop steward system operated in much the same way as in other engineering establishments.

For the most part during the war, there grew up, side by side with the District Councils movement, a second type of semi-official organization within the N.U.R. This is known as the ' Grade Movement '. The National Union of Railwaymen, although it does not include the clerical grades or the majority of the locomotive or supervisory grades on the railways, has from the first aimed at being an ' all-grades ' Union, including in its ranks all sorts of railway workers. In its constitution it accords a limited degree of representation to a few big departments, or groups of grades ; but on the whole the object of its founders was to subordinate, rather than to emphasize, grade differences. This led to the formation, on an unofficial basis, of numerous national or local grade ' Vigilance Committees ' or ' Line Committees ', which aimed at watching over the interests of a particular section of railway workers and ensuring that the grievances of that section should receive prompt and proper attention from the Union as a whole. Gradually this grade organization, originally framed upon and still regarded as laying undue emphasis on sectional differences by the more dogmatic ' Industrial Unionists ', has achieved a considerable measure of Trade Union recognition, and has come to be consulted and referred to by the Union Executive when the grievances of a particular grade are under consideration. Official Grade Conferences have been called by the Union ; and the grade organizations have also called at times unofficial conferences of their own, and have threatened strike action even without the authorization of their Union.

These grade organizations, again, are not, strictly speaking, formed upon a workshop basis. But they tend to have their own local representatives in each operating unit, and these representatives very largely fulfil the function of shop stewards. The unofficial railway movement has hitherto been kept, partly no doubt because it is not so much ' unofficial ' as ' semi-official ', somewhat unrelated to the ' rank and file ' movements in other industries. It is, however, essentially on the same lines, and sets out to satisfy largely the same needs as workshop organization serves in industries which are operated on a factory basis. It would be clearly impossible, in most branches of the railway service, to reproduce more nearly the exact conditions of the shop stewards' movement in, say, the engineering industry.

It would be possible to say something of minor developments of ' workshop ' or similar organization which have taken place in a number of other industries. But the examples which have already been given seem to indicate clearly enough what has been the general line of development. The ' workshop ', strictly speaking, exists only in those industries which are carried on in factories. But almost everywhere modern methods of large-scale production and transport involve the concentration in a single place of work, and the co-operation upon a single group of activities, of a band of men who thus acquire common interest and a capacity for action in common. These units vary much from case to case ; but almost everywhere— in the dock, the pit, the railway station, the bus garage or tramway dépôt, the warehouse, and so on, there is some equivalent to the workshop which is capable of forming the nucleus of an organization. The extent to which new forms of Trade Union activity have grown up around these units during

the war varies ; but on the whole the growth has been remarkable, though it is difficult to measure in the absence of rules,
reports, or documents of any kind describing the majority of
its manifestations. This chapter must be taken as indicating
the general character of its war-time growth ; but it must be
remembered that this growth was throughout experimental,
and that hard and fast constitutional forms have, in most cases,
been so far absent from these developments of working class
co-operative activity.

CHAPTER XIII

WORKSHOP ORGANIZATION UNDER THE
WHITLEY REPORT

On the 8th of March 1917 the first Whitley Report was issued. This had been drawn up by a special Sub-Committee of the Government Reconstruction Committee appointed in 1916; but the Sub-Committee became in 1917 a Committee acting under the newly created Ministry of Reconstruction. The main proposals of the first Whitley Report fall outside the scope of this study, and need only be very briefly outlined for our purpose. The employers, Trade Unionists, and Government representatives who formed the Committee proposed that, in all strongly organized industries, the existing facilities for negotiation and discussion should be enlarged, and that there should be established Joint Standing Industrial Councils, consisting of employers' and Trade Union representatives in equal numbers. These councils were intended to be more than mere bargaining or negotiating bodies. They were to discuss all problems of common concern to the industry, and to usher in a régime of harmonious co-operation between employers and employed. They were to be recognized by the Government as representing the industries concerned, and were represented as satisfying the workers' claim to a share in 'control'. It is beyond the scope of this study to discuss the actual effects of their establishment.

Subordinate to the National Industrial Councils there were to be District Councils, and under these again joint Works Committees in each particular establishment. In making this proposal, the Committee wrote as follows:

13. In the well-organized industries, one of the first questions to be considered should be the establishment of local and works organizations to supplement and make more effective the work of the central bodies. It is not enough to secure co-operation at the centre between the national organizations; it is equally necessary to enlist the activity

and support of employers and employed in the districts and in individual establishments. The National Industrial Council should not be regarded as complete in itself ; what is needed is a triple organization—in the workshops, the districts, and nationally. Moreover, it is essential that the organization at each of these three stages should proceed on a common principle, and that the greatest measure of common action between them should be secured.

14. With this end in view, we are of opinion that the following proposals should be laid before the National Industrial Councils :

(a) That District Councils, representative of the Trade Unions and of the Employers' Association in the industry, should be created, or developed out of the existing machinery for negotiation in the various trades.

(b) That Works Committees, representative of the management and of the workers employed, should be instituted in particular works to act in close co-operation with the district and national machinery.

As it is of the highest importance that the scheme making provision for these Committees should be such as to secure the support of the Trade Unions and Employers' Associations concerned, its design should be a matter for agreement between these organizations.

Just as regular meetings and continuity of co-operation are essential in the case of the National Industrial Councils, so they seem to be necessary in the case of the district and works organizations. The object is to secure co-operation by granting to workpeople a greater share in the consideration of matters affecting their industry, and this can only be achieved by keeping employers and workpeople in constant touch.

15. The respective functions of Works Committees, District Councils, and National Councils will no doubt require to be determined separately in accordance with the varying conditions of different industries. Care will need to be taken in each case to delimit accurately their respective functions, in order to avoid overlapping and resulting friction. For instance, where conditions of employment are determined by national agreements, the District Councils or Works Committees should not be allowed to contract out of conditions so laid down, nor, where conditions are determined by local agreements, should such power be allowed to Works Committees.

These recommendations of the first Whitley Report were further explained and expanded in the ' Supplementary Report on Works Committees ', issued by the same Committee in the winter of 1917.[1] In this Report no attempt was made to lay

---

[1] For full text, see Appendix E.

down a precise or formal constitution for Works Committees, the exact character of which, it was held, would necessarily vary from industry to industry. Stress was, however, laid on the fact that the joint machinery proposed in the first Report would be essentially incomplete unless full provision was made for joint workshop bodies, and unless these bodies were definitely linked up with the National and District Joint Councils to be established under the Whitley scheme. Such a linking-up, it was urged, necessarily involved at least two things : (1) that the Works Committee should act definitely within the national and local agreements entered into by the Trade Unions and Employers' Associations, and should not attempt to deal with any question which was properly a matter for collective bargaining over an area wider than that of the individual establishment ; and (2) that only Trade Unionists should be represented on the workers' side of the Committees, and that this Trade Union representation should be on a basis agreed upon with the Trade Unions themselves. Attention was specially drawn to the ' danger that Works Committees might be used, or be thought to be used, in opposition to Trade Unionism '. This, it was pointed out, would be fatal to the objects which the Whitley Committee had in view. No encouragement of any kind was given to the idea, sometimes put forward by particular groups of employers, that the constitution of Works Committees might provide a bulwark against the growth of Trade Unionism, and render it unnecessary for the employers to recognize the Unions. It was made clear that the whole scheme was based upon the fullest recognition, both in the workshops and over the wider areas, of Trade Union collective bargaining.

At the beginning of 1919 the Ministry of Labour issued, in pamphlet form, as Number 4 of its series of ' Industrial Reports ' bearing upon the Whitley scheme,[1] its notes and suggestions for the constitution of National and District Councils, and of Works Committees, on the lines laid down by the Whitley Committee. The points referred to above were

[1] For text of section dealing with Works Committees, see Appendix F.

again strongly emphasized in these suggestions. It was stated that the workshop machinery must be in ' the closest possible connexion ' with the District and National Councils, and that anything done in the workshops ' must be consistent with the principles of the collective agreements accepted by the District and National Authorities '. It was further stated that ' the members of the workers' side should be Trade Union representatives.[1] The Minister of Labour also went into considerable further detail concerning the constitution, functions, and procedure of the proposed Committees.

The first report of the Whitley Committee was placed before the Cabinet, and was by it approved in the autumn of 1917. A circular letter was then issued by the Ministry of Labour, calling upon employers' associations and Trade Unions in the various industries to take the action necessary in order to bring the proposed machinery into being, in so far as it was applicable to their particular industries under the terms of the Reports. A special department was set up at the Ministry of Labour, and entrusted with the task of forming Whitley Councils, or, where full Whitley Councils could not be created, ' Interim Joint Reconstruction Committees ' which, it was hoped, would grow later into fully fledged Whitley Councils. At the same time, while it urged upon the private employers the acceptance of the Whitley Report, the Government, despite considerable pressure from some of the principal Trade Unions concerned, for a long time refused to apply it in any form to the industrial enterprises under its own control, or to the Civil Service. It was not until 1919 that the Government at last yielded, and agreed to the setting up of Whitley machinery in the Civil Service, the Royal Dockyards, the Post Office, and among other groups of State employees.

This is not the place to tell the full story of the Whitley Reports, and of the efforts made to apply them throughout industry. In general, it may be said that, although numerous Joint Standing Industrial Councils were created, a great many of these were for small or comparatively unorganized industries,

[1] For explanation and qualifications, see full text in Appendix F.

and the majority of the biggest industries stood aloof from the new development, and preferred to retain their pre-war machinery of conference or conciliation. The miners, the railwaymen, the engineering and shipbuilding workers, and the cotton operatives were among the groups which preferred their own methods to those put forward by the Whitley Committee. A few important industries—building, waterside transport, tramways and wool among them—set up Councils ; but the principal welcome to the Reports from the Trade Union side came from the big general labour Unions which had organized many of the workers in the smaller and more scattered industries. In many such industries or quasi-industries, Councils were set up, although clearly their establishment in these cases had not been contemplated by the signatories to the Whitley Reports. ' Needles and fishhooks ', ' coir matting ', ' zinc and spelter ', and ' furniture removing ', are hardly ' industries' in the sense contemplated in the original Reports.

It was also a notable fact that, while the Reports had laid very great stress on the importance of works and workshop machinery as part of the organization to be established, the great majority of the Whitley Councils which were set up took no steps at all to stimulate the formation of Works Committees. In a number of cases no District Councils were established, and in very few was any real attempt made to secure the co-ordination of machinery at the three stages—works, local, and national. In 1921 very few of the Joint Industrial Councils had set up any regular works machinery at all, and the majority of these appeared to possess little life, and to be consulted only on a very restricted number of questions, of which the most important have so far been the training of ex-soldiers and various aspects of welfare work. It seems to be generally admitted, that, whatever degree of success or failure may be credited to the National Joint Industrial Councils, the proposals for joint workshop organization have been almost completely abortive, only a few isolated employers, such as Messrs. Cadbury, Messrs. Rowntree, and Messrs. Pascall, having even attempted to take seriously this part of the Whitley Reports.

This failure is, no doubt, partly accounted for by opposition on the side of the employers. When the Whitley Reports were first produced, the Federation of British Industries lost no time in declaring, in a communication to its constituent bodies, its hostility to joint works or workshop committees of the type proposed. This hostility was not, indeed, directed against joint works committees of any sort, but against the granting to such bodies of any industrial functions at all. It was the essence of the Whitley scheme that the committees which it proposed should have industrial functions, and the opposition of many employers to this goes a long way towards accounting for the failure to get them established.

It is, however, also the case that the Trade Union shop stewards were often most reluctant to exchange the *de facto* recognition which they had secured for their own purely Trade Union committees for the new form of organization proposed in the Whitley Reports. They often held that they could secure better results for their members by preserving their complete independence, and only meeting the management when a question calling for joint consideration arose. Thus, in the majority of cases, neither party pressed for the creation of works or workshop machinery under the terms of the Reports; and it was therefore inevitable that these sections of them should fall largely into abeyance.

This is true in the case of most privately owned industries in which Whitley Councils were established. The position was, however, somewhat different when the Government was at last induced to assent to the setting up of Joint Councils with the employees of the State. Thus, when in 1919 the Reports were applied to the industrial establishments of the State and to the Civil Service, the workshop or equivalent machinery occupied an important place in the special schemes which were devised. Under the Civil Service Whitley Council were set up special Councils or Committees for the employees of each Government Department, and sometimes for particular branches of a department. These Departmental Councils or Committees resembled the Works Councils of big industrial establishments.

In the case of the Postal Service, which was represented in the main Council for the whole Civil Service, two separate Whitley Councils were set up, one for the Engineering Department and the other for the manipulative departments of the Post Office, and, under each of these Departmental Councils was a regular system of Office, as well as District, Committees. This machinery has not worked well; for the 'staff' sides of the various Civil Service Whitley Councils complain that the 'official' sides persist in treating them as mere deputations, and allow them no real influence over policy, sheltering always behind the Minister or the central control exercised by the Treasury over the whole Service when the 'staff' sides desire to discuss really controversial questions. The machinery, however, has been created; and it would still be premature to pass any final judgement on its utility or success.

In the Royal Dockyards the Whitley scheme was finally installed during the year 1919. The great majority of the Dockyard employees are enrolled in engineering, shipyard, or general labour Unions, most of whose members are in private employment. There had been, before the Whitley Reports, a keen desire on the part of the Dockyard members of these Unions to secure special representative machinery within their Unions, in order that their industrial interests, which, owing to the peculiar conditions of Dockyard service, differed considerably from those of other engineering and shipyard workers, might receive special and expert attention. This had led to the growth of the shop stewards' movement in the Dockyards, and to the creation, by some of the Unions, and especially by the Amalgamated Society of Engineers, of Dockyard Advisory Councils. The Whitley scheme was welcomed by many Dockyard workers as a means of placing this special machinery on a firmer foundation; and, after conferences between the Admiralty and the Trade Unions concerned, an elaborate system of shop, yard, and trade committees was devised, and applied to all the Royal Dockyards and similar establishments, the whole machinery being co-ordinated in a single Whitley Council representing all the industrial establishments owned and administered by the State.

The main distinction between this Dockyard machinery and the forms of workshop organization adopted elsewhere lay in the establishment of a dual system of committees. The machinery established for each Dockyard and for each department within it followed the customary lines of works and workshop organization ; but the special interests of each trade were left to be looked after by Trade Committees, to which all purely ' trade ' questions arising in the yards were exclusively referred in the first instance. If the Trade Committees could not deal successfully with any question, it was then referred to the Trade Union concerned, which would take the matter up directly with the Dockyard authorities, or with the Admiralty itself. This machinery is still in operation, and seems, on the whole, to be working fairly well. Both Yard and Trade Committees have been largely concerned in the negotiations which have been necessary for the regulation of short time working and of the heavy discharges which have taken place since the end of the war.[1]

It will be seen that, except in cases in which the State itself is the employer, workshop machinery has played only an insignificant part in the developments following upon the Whitley Reports. If the Reports themselves had been more of a success in their practical application, a serious attempt would probably have been made to give effect to their provisions for workshop machinery. But in fact the Whitley Councils have, in nearly all cases, quite failed to realize the large promises with which they were inaugurated. There is nothing that clearly differentiates most of them from the numerous Boards of Conciliation, Joint Committees, and Conferences which were already in existence before the war. Even the few councils, such as the Pottery Council and the ' Builders' Parliament ',[2] which set out with big schemes for

[1] See Appendix G for full text of the scheme for the application of the Whitley Reports to the Royal Dockyards.

[2] The ' Builders' Parliament ' was a body similar in structure to the Whitley Councils, but with somewhat wider functions. It was founded quite apart from the Whitley scheme, but was subsequently recognized by the Ministry of Labour as the Joint Industrial Council for the Building Industry. Its existence has now

the re-organization of their industries, have shrunk back from their original ambitions, and became either functionless, or just like any other form of negotiating machinery between employers and Trade Unions. Judged by its pretensions, the whole Whitley scheme has broken down; and nowhere is its failure more obvious and complete than in the sphere of work-shop organization.

(October, 1922) just been terminated by the withdrawal of the National Federation of Building Trade Employers; but provision is being made for the continuance of certain of its sub-committees.

CHAPTER XIV

THE WORKSHOP MOVEMENT AND THE END
OF THE WAR

THE extent to which the conclusion of military operations
between the Allied and Associated Powers and those of Central
Europe altered the conditions under which the workshop
movement had to operate has already been mentioned more
than once. The movement, as we have seen, owed its rapid
rise to influence mainly to two things—the immense number
of workshop problems to which the changes in product and
methods of production, and the constant draining away of
men for military service, gave rise, and the war-time disarmament of the official Trade Union organizations. The cessation
of recruiting and of the production of war requisites which
followed the armistice did not, indeed, at once cause these
problems to lapse. Workshops which had been adapted to
war purposes had to be re-organized to suit the purposes of
peace ; and the numerous pledges given by the Government
and the employers that Trade Union customs and conditions,
abrogated during the war, should be restored as soon as hostilities were over, fell due for fulfilment. The men returning from
the army, hale or disabled, had to be reinstated in industry ;
and something had to be done to train the numerous young
men whose industrial training had been either interrupted or
omitted because of the demands of ' national service ' during
the war.

It had been supposed, before the war actually ended, that
this change-over from war to peace conditions would involve,
and be attended by, almost as much friction as the changes
which were gradually introduced during the war period.
Contrary to almost all expectations, it was rapidly, and almost
smoothly, carried out. Friction arose, in particular cases, over

both the ' restoration of Trade Union customs ', which was carried out under the sanction of a special Act of Parliament, and the conditions of employment of ex-service men.   But, taken as a whole, the transition was extraordinarily rapid, and was accomplished with relatively little friction.   It had been prophesied, by many different authorities, that the effect of the war-time experience would be a permanent revolution in the methods of British engineering practice ;   and that the methods of mass production, which had been successfully applied to many peace-time engineering products, with the result that the labour-power of the skilled workers would become a drug in the market, and a vast new demand for the labour of less skilled workers would be perpetuated.   In fact, however, even if a revolution of this type is on the way, no such developments have at present taken place.   The engineering employers have, for the most part, reverted largely to their pre-war methods of production ;   and the unskilled munition workers have discovered that they have far more to fear in the way of post-war unemployment than the skilled men in the industries affected.

In the restoration of pre-war practices which occurred during 1919, the shop stewards and their organizations played their part, drawing attention to the practices which the employers were under an obligation to restore, and often entering into negotiations, on a workshop basis, concerning the form and method of restoration.   They also played some part in connexion with the application in the various works of the scheme for the training and re-employment of ex-soldiers who were partially disabled, and in the readjustments of factory conditions which followed upon the lowering of hours that took place in most trades in 1919.   But none of these activities was, as a rule, likely to lead to particularly aggressive or to unofficial action by the shop stewards' movement ;   and, during the period immediately following upon the conclusion of the war, there is no doubt that the movement lost a good deal of its aggressive and militant character.   This loss was accentuated, both by the fact that the official Trade Unions had, to a great extent, recovered their freedom of action, and by the activity of many employers, when the change from war to peace conditions afforded an opportunity, in discharging those stewards who had shown the most militant disposition, and in breaking up groups of stewards who had become accustomed to common action during the war years.

In consequence of the changed conditions, the shop stewards' movement, in the form in which it had grown to notoriety and power, gradually melted away when the conditions which had favoured its activity were removed. Some of the less vigorous Workers' Committees speedily disappeared altogether, and most of the others were greatly reduced in strength. Their loose form of organization, described in previous chapters, rendered them peculiarly liable to rapid accretions and diminutions of power; and, under the changed conditions, a great deal of their support inevitably fell away. The unsuccessful strikes on the Clyde and in Belfast in the spring of 1919, in which the demand was for a forty-hour week in the former and for a forty-four hour week in the latter district, were the last big attempts at aggressive industrial action by the war-time shop stewards' movement. In both cases, failure hastened the process of dissolution.

This is not to say that the Workers' Committees were in most cases dissolved, or that the unofficial shop stewards' movement ceased to exist. Both the local Workers' Committees and the federal ' National Shop Stewards' and Workers' Committee ' remained in existence; but they were reduced during 1919 to purely skeleton organizations, to which only those who went all the way with their ' left-wing ' Socialist ideas remained faithful. The large number of sympathizers who had gathered round the few militants during the war years for the most part fell away, and at the end of 1919 the entire dissolution of the unofficial movement, and the continuation of the shop steward system on a purely official basis, seemed to be probable.

That this did not occur was almost wholly the consequence of the Russian Revolution. Deprived of its industrial oppor-

tunities and reduced once more to an organization in which
the extreme left-wing minority alone was enrolled, the movement acquired more and more a definitely political character.
During the year 1920 a revival began, but the new movement
was in many respects different from the old. It was no longer
a body of workshop leaders emerging from the rank and file
for the purpose of dealing with immediate industrial grievances,
but a left-wing organization possessing a definitely revolutionary purpose and looking, more than at any time during
the war, to Moscow for its inspiration. At first it had no clear
or organized connexion with the Communist movement ; but,
in the course of the year, not only was a Communist Party
formed in Great Britain, but also a British Provisional Committee of the Red (or Moscow) Trade Union International.
With this the remnants of the unofficial shop stewards' movement became definitely connected ; and the movement itself
was thus absorbed into, and became a part, though still an
autonomous part, of British Communist organization.

During the war the effective centre of attention in the
Trade Union movement was in the engineering and kindred
industries. Immediately the war was over, the centre shifted
to the mining industry. In 1918 the Miners' Federation of
Great Britain had defined its fundamental demands as including
both nationalization and the concession of an effective share
in the control of the mines to the organized workers. At the
beginning of 1919 a threatened national strike of miners, in
connexion with these and other demands, was averted by the
establishment of the Royal Commission on the Coal Industry,
before which the miners elaborated demands including the
establishment of a representative Mining Council, and of Coalfield and Pit Committees, to which the actual management
of the industry under public ownership should be entrusted.
The refusal of the Government, despite the recommendations
of a majority of the Commission, including the Chairman,
Sir John Sankey, to grant either nationalization or a share
in control, has since kept the industry in a condition of permanent unrest.

This unrest was favourable to the growth of the unofficial movements which had already sprung up among the miners during the war period.[1] Fresh rank and file committees were formed in the coalfields, and those which were in existence gained fresh adherents. Finally, at the end of 1920, the local unofficial bodies drew together into a national body, which assumed the name of the Mine-workers' Section of the Workers' Committee Movement. It is difficult to estimate the strength of the bodies of which this movement is composed; but they undoubtedly possess a considerable backing in many of the coalfields, and particularly in South Wales and the west of Scotland. They too have become actively connected with the propaganda of Communism, and have taken a prominent part in furthering the British agitation in favour of the ' Red ' Trade Union International.

The tendencies which were already at work during the war period made the growth of purely revolutionary agitation among the unofficial industrial organizations based on the workshops inevitable. Shrinkage due to the passing of war conditions and the growth and recognition under the Shop Stewards' Agreement [2] of official Trade Union stewards and workshop bodies left the unofficial movement consisting almost wholly of definitely ' left-wing ' elements, which naturally responded at once to the call of Moscow. There were no longer obvious daily workshop problems on which it was essential for stewards to concentrate, whatever their opinions on the wider issues of Labour policy might be. Consequently, there was not the same obvious and immediate need for workshop solidarity. It was a time when there was little action in immediate prospect; and accordingly, there was nothing to restrain the development of theoretical differences. The unofficial shop stewards' movement ceased to count, or to desire to count, in daily workshop affairs, and came to regard itself mainly as the pioneer of the revolutionary spirit in the workshops. This was less the case in the mining industry, where there were big immediate issues

[1] See ante, Chapter XII.
[2] See ante, Chapter VIII.

to be faced ; but it was very much the case in the engineering shops, which were most of all affected, and diminished in relative importance, by the cessation of hostilities.

It is not part of the purpose of this study to deal with these post-war developments, except to the slight extent to which they must be mentioned in order to round off the history of the war period. I have therefore treated them very concisely, although they present many features of interest to the student of Trade Union problems. Their history belongs, however, more properly to the history of the British revolutionary movement than to that of the industrial forms of workshop organization.

CHAPTER XV

THE POSSIBILITIES OF WORKSHOP ORGANIZATION

THROUGHOUT this study the reader will have perceived that the most critical problem of workshop organization, from the standpoint of the Labour movement, is that of the relation between official Trade Unionism, with its national, district, and branch machinery, and the grouping of workers round a particular factory or place of employment. We have seen that, in the majority of industries, the branch organization of Trade Unionism takes no account of the factory or similar industrial unit, and groups men in accordance rather with their place of residence than with their place of employment. It is only where, as in the mining industry, there is a necessary tendency for the two to coincide, or where, as in the London Society of Compositors, there is no branch organization at all, that the unit of the place of employment finds natural expression through the official Trade Union machinery.

The recognition of the workshop as a unit of Trade Union organization would undoubtedly have been sooner and more easily achieved had it not been for rivalry and overlapping between Trade Unions. Where there are rival Unions seeking to organize the same classes of workers in a shop, the feeling of solidarity among the workers in the shop is thwarted, and the sectional loyalty to each particular Trade Union prevents the easy growth of a capacity for common action by the workshop as a whole. This was particularly the common experience in the engineering and kindred industries before the war ; and the rivalry among Trade Unions explains why an exceptional stimulus was needed before workshop organization could achieve any considerable measure of recognition, despite the obvious suitability of the productive conditions.

We have seen how the conditions created by the war

provided this stimulus, and how workshop organization, in many different forms, sprang spontaneously into existence during the war period. We have noted, too, that the disarmament of the official Trade Unions by the Munitions Acts and other war-time measures made it inevitable that the new developments should assume to some extent an unofficial character, and facilitated the rise of purely unofficial bodies, such as the Workers' Committees, which were based on ideas involving a challenge to the more orthodox conceptions of Trade Union leadership. We have watched this unofficial movement, which owed its rise mainly to industrial causes and actual workshop grievances and problems, assuming more and more a political character, and finally passing over into the industrial organization of the Communist movement.

But meanwhile, as we have also seen, the shop steward system had secured definite recognition, on a permanent basis, both from the Trade Unions and from the employers. With the revision of the Trade Union rules [1] so as to provide for the exercise of certain industrial functions by the shop stewards and shop committees, and, in the case of the Amalgamated Engineering Union, also to a small extent for the direct representation of shop stewards on the Trade Union District Committees, the system entered upon a new phase, and became free, within limits, to develop under official Trade Union auspices. The Shop Stewards' Agreement of 1919,[1] unsatisfactory as it was in certain respects, registered the acquiescence of the engineering employers in this development, and, in conjunction with the measures taken by the Unions themselves, ensured the permanence and stability of the shop steward system. However much the advocates of unofficial shop stewardism may criticize the ' officialization ' of the movement, and deplore the loss of revolutionary spirit resulting from official recognition, there is no doubt that these measures have ensured the permanence of a system which might otherwise have rapidly disappeared when the peculiar stimulus to which it was a response no longer remained active.

[1] See *ante,* Chapter VIII.

The unofficial Workers' Committees may, or may not, prove to be of permanent importance in the history of revolutionary agitation. But, so far as purely industrial functions are concerned, it is clearly the official steward, duly recognized by his Trade Union and by the employer, who will play the more important part in the workshop movement towards industrial democracy. The way for the development of the official shop steward system has been made already a good deal easier by the amalgamation of a number of the most important Societies of skilled engineering workers to form the Amalgamated Engineering Union. This big Union, formed in 1920, includes, besides the Amalgamated Society of Engineers, most of the Societies which were its serious rivals in the enrolment of skilled workers in the general engineering trades. This amalgamation has removed the need for a great deal of the useless and friction-causing duplication of shop stewards representing the same classes of workers—a duplication which was almost inevitable as long as the old sectionalism and rivalry between Societies continued to exist. The engineering amalgamation, indeed, included only the skilled workers, and by no means the whole of these. But it did mean that, in future, the spectacle of two Unions organizing workers of precisely the same classes in one factory would be exceptional ; and it did mean that the separate groups of shop stewards whom each Union had in many cases maintained in one and the same establishment, were replaced by a single group, responsible to a single Trade Union, and capable of common action.

Thus, the experience of the war period has not been thrown away, and a permanent mark has been left on the structure of Trade Unionism in the industries principally affected by the war-time developments. But it remains to be seen how deep this mark will be, and to what degree of importance the shop steward system will attain as an integral and recognized part of Trade Union organization. We have seen Mr. Murphy in his pamphlet on ' The Workers' Committee ', contrasting the vitality and industrial capacity of the workshop branch with the inertia and sectionalism of the present Trade Union branch organization, based on habitation rather than place of work.[1] How far will the recognition of the shop steward system lead to a gradual supersession of the branch by the workshop unit, and thus realize, within the official Trade Union bodies, the structure which the leaders of the Workers' Committees sought to improvise apart from them ? It is at least possible that, even if the branch in its present form remains for a long time as the nominal unit of organization, it will be definitely superseded, for industrial purposes, by the works meeting and the Works Committee, and that the District Committees, to whose hands the local control of Trade Union policy is now entrusted, will come to consist mainly of shop stewards, representing industrial units, rather than of branch delegates, as at present.

The extent to which this constitutional development of Trade Unionism takes place will, no doubt, depend mainly on the actual functions which are successfully undertaken by the shop stewards and other workshop organizations. If these can show their capacity to assume important industrial functions, and to realize, within their sphere of operation, something of the Trade Union demand for ' workers' control in industry ', increased recognition for them in Trade Union government will follow almost as a matter of course, whereas no constitutional readjustment will make the workshop system of organization a practical success unless the workshop leaders themselves plainly demonstrate their capacity for power.

The most significant, from this point of view, of the ideas which developed among the workshop leaders during the war period is that which is usually known by the name of ' Collective Contract ', or, in other words, a plan under which the workers in each shop, under the auspices of their Unions, would enter into a collective contract with their employer to produce for an agreed price the required output, and would themselves undertake the organization of the shop and the necessary discipline and supervision. This was first adumbrated, perhaps even before the outbreak of war, and certainly in 1914 and 1915, by the Guild Socialists ; but it was developed further, and given

[1] See Chapter X.

a more practical shape, by various bodies of shop stewards, apparently acting to a large extent independently, in different parts of the country. The first definite exposition of the proposal was contained in the memorandum, entitled ' Towards Industrial Democracy ', which was published by the Paisley Trades Council early in 1917. This was written in collaboration by Mr. J. Paton, a chief steward at a big munition works on the Clyde, and a leader in the Guild Socialist movement, and by Mr. W. Gallacher, of the Clyde Workers' Committee, one of the most active men in the unofficial workshop movement.[1] Almost at the same time, another body of stewards, who had formed themselves into the ' Weymouth Industrial Research Group ', began the issue of a series of papers expounding the same idea. This group, the most important of whose memoranda is appended to this study,[2] afterwards became the Weymouth Group of the National Guilds League. The Guild Socialists were, throughout, the most active propagandists of the idea of ' Collective Contract ', although the plan was accepted by many in whose minds it had no basis in a definite social or industrial theory.

' Collective Contract ' arose as an attempt to deal, in a way which would relate it definitely to the demand for ' workers' control in industry ', with one of the most difficult and pressing problems of engineering Trade Unionism. We have seen how, during the war period, constant attempts were being made, usually in face of the opposition of the skilled workers, to replace the time-work system of payment by one form or another of payment by results. The advocates of Collective Contract usually urged that a merely negative attitude of opposition to payment by results could not be effective, and could at most only retard its introduction. It was, however, as they believed, possible to turn the demand for payment by results to the positive advantage of the workers, by using it as an instrument for the winning of workshop control. This could be done if, instead of insisting on the retention of the time-work

---

[1] See Appendix H.   [2] See Appendix J.

system of payment, the workers demanded the substitution for the individual relation at present recognized between the firm and each employee, of a collective relation between the firm and the whole organized group of workers employed in a particular shop or department. Let the workers, represented by their committee of shop stewards, go to the management with the proposition that the whole group should enter into a ' collective contract ' with the firm to produce for an agreed price the whole output required. If such contract were made, the advocates of the system contended, the need for individual bargaining between the firm and the worker, and for the constant disputes which now arise over particular piece-work prices, would disappear. The price at which the output of the shop could be produced would be determined by collective bargaining, and the sum agreed upon would be paid over in a lump to the Shop Committee, which would be responsible for its division, on principles laid down by the Trade Unions, among the workers concerned. With the disappearance of the personal wage-relationship between the firm and each individual employee, the need for a workshop discipline imposed by the employer would also cease, and the organized group of workers would be free, within the general conditions laid down by the Trade Unions, to determine its own methods of workshop management, to appoint its own supervisors, and itself to arrange for the distribution and execution of work in the shop. The shop itself, the machinery, and the materials would still be provided by the employer, and the product would still be his to dispose of as he might think fit, the workers merely converting the material for him at an agreed price. But a whole sphere of industrial control—that of workshop organization—would have been transferred from the present management to the workers organized as a group on a workshop basis.

Further results would necessarily follow from the adoption of this system. Clearly, the engagement and dismissal of workers, any necessary arrangement for short-time working or overtime, and other similar questions now under the employers' control would in future be dealt with by the Works Committee

F*

acting under the Trade Unions to which their members belonged. A firm foothold would have been found for the system of workers' control, even without any overthrow or dispossession of capitalism.

Of course, most of the advocates of ' Collective Contract ' regarded it as merely a first step. It had, from the standpoint of those who were aiming at a complete but gradual transformation of the industrial system, the manifest advantage of providing for a gradual transference of power and responsibility to the organized workers, and of giving them in the sphere of the control which they would be immediately called upon to assume, experience which would be of the greatest value in fitting them for the acquisition of a wider control at a later stage. ' Encroaching control ' was the name often given by the Guild Socialists to the policy of which ' Collective Contract ' was one of the practical expressions.

The system outlined above was nowhere during the war, and has been nowhere up to the present time, fully installed, although there has been a great deal of discussion of it, and something very like it is in operation at some ports, particularly in Ireland and the Bristol Channel, for certain types of waterside transport. During the war numerous munition firms adopted, as we have seen, various collective systems of payment by results, under which a bonus, calculated on the output of a whole shop or department, was paid to all workers, either equally or in proportion to their time-rates. Sometimes a special Shop Committee was appointed, or an existing Shop Stewards' Committee utilized, for the purpose of supervising the administration of such schemes ; and some of these committees secured in practice a considerable direct control over the organization of the shop. An even nearer approach was made in certain Clyde shops, and a system closely resembling ' Collective Contract ' was for a time actually in operation at a big South Coast munition works. The history of this experiment is interesting. It resulted in increased output, and appears to have been very popular among the younger men in the works. But it was discontinued because of the resistance to it of certain of the older men, who complained that it took away their chance of high individual piece-work earnings, by spreading the earnings on the whole output more evenly over the whole of the workers in the shop.

The number of experiments is too small, and the evidence concerning them too scanty, to make it possible, on the strength of them, to draw any positive conclusions as to the success of the ' Collective Contract ' system. It has been partly adopted in certain branches of the transport industry in Wales since the conclusion of the war ; but in the engineering and kindred industries the circumstances have been unfavourable, and, although it has been largely discussed, both over the industry as a whole and in such special branches as scientific and optical instrument making, nothing appears to have been done to secure its adoption. The decisive rejection by the engineers, in 1920, of a proposal to permit the general introduction of payment by results, while it did not prevent the gradual extension of the system, rendered difficult attempts at collective regulation of it by the Trade Unions. Moreover, the trade depression and still more the defeat of the Trade Unions in the national engineering lock-out of 1922, put an end for the time to all forward movements among the workers in the engineering industry.

It seems clear that, if the war-time developments of workshop organization are to provide the basis for permanent adjustments of the industrial system, it is in the sphere of ' workshop control ' that its achievements will have to be made. The abnormal shortage of labour during the war, and the impossibility of making the changes connected with dilution effective unless a considerable measure of co-operation could be secured from the skilled workers already in the shops, placed these workers for the time in an exceptionally strong position, and enabled them to take up an attitude of independence which would certainly not have been tolerated in other circumstances, and to assume a considerable degree of control over the administration of the shops. These favourable conditions, of course, ceased to exist when the war ended ; and accordingly much of the newly won power and responsibility of the shop stewards and workshop bodies was lost. If the experiments made, and the experience gained, during the war period are to be utilized as the basis of permanent industrial changes, this will be done only by a far more painful and difficult reconquest of ground which has been won and lost already. This reconquest, moreover, will involve the far more deliberate pursuit by the Trade Unions, and by the workshop bodies acting under them, of a conscious policy designed to bring about an actual transference of control and responsibility. It is difficult at present to say how far or how fast the Trade Unions are moving in this direction; for the advance of Communism has, for the moment, kicked up a revolutionary dust which hides the movement of more purely industrial forces and ideas. Certainly, there has been a set-back from the high hopes entertained by the younger leaders of Labour during the war years; but such a set-back was rendered inevitable by the changed conditions in industry itself. The war-time developments have, for the present, spent their force; and the time has come when it is possible to attempt—as I have attempted in this study—to take stock of them, and to give some account, both of their positive achievements and of the ideas which animated those who were mainly responsible for them, and are still animating this same ' conscious minority ' in the ranks of Labour which is working by one means or another for a complete transformation of the industrial system.

APPENDIX A

COVENTRY ENGINEERING JOINT COMMITTEE

SHOP RULES AND INSTRUCTIONS FOR STEWARDS

(See Chapter V)

The rules drawn up by the Coventry Engineering Joint Committee, representing practically all the Trade Unions with members in the engineering shops in the district, are here given both because they include all the normal regulations for the activities of recognized Trade Union shop stewards, and because they include certain features which are not typical. The duties prescribed are much the same in Coventry as in other districts : the difference is that, whereas in most areas each Trade Union has its separate shop stewards, imperfectly co-ordinated through the Joint Committee, in Coventry all recognized stewards hold the card of the Joint Committee itself, and are appointed to represent their trade or shop, without distinction of Union. I cannot find that precisely this system was in force anywhere else, although there were approximations to it. It should be mentioned that there was also in Coventry an unofficial shop stewards' movement and a Workers' Committee not recognized by the Engineering Joint Committee.

1. That the Coventry Engineering Joint Committee shall be the Executive Committee over all shop stewards and Works Committees affiliated. Any change of practice in any shop or works must receive the consent of the Joint Engineering Committee before being accepted by the men concerned.

2. That all nominees for shop stewards must be members of Societies affiliated to the C.E.J.C.

3. Stewards shall be elected by ballot for a term not exceeding six months ; all retiring stewards to be eligible for re-election.

4. Each section shall be able to elect a steward, irrespective of Society.

5. The stewards of each department shall elect a chief steward.

6. The chief stewards of departments shall constitute the Works Committee, who, if exceeding twelve in number, can appoint an Executive Committee of seven, including Chairman and Secretary.

7. All stewards shall have an official steward's card issued by the Joint Committee.

8. Each steward on being elected, and the same endorsed by his Society, the Joint Committee Secretary shall send him an official card.

9. The steward must examine any man's membership card who starts in the shop in his section. He should then advise the man to report to his respective Secretary, and give him any information required on rates and conditions, &c. There shall be a show of cards every month to ascertain if every member is a sound member, and if any member is in arrears eight weeks he must report same to the chief steward.

10. If there is any doubt of any man not receiving the district rate of wages the steward can demand to examine pay ticket.

11. Any member accepting a price or time basis for a job must hand record of same to his section steward, who shall keep a record of times and prices on his section of any work, and hand the same to chief shop steward.

12. The chief steward shall keep a record of all times and prices recorded to him by sections of his department. On a section being not represented he shall see to the election of steward for such section.

13. Any grievance arising on any section must be reported to chief shop steward, who shall, with steward of section and man concerned, interview foreman or manager. Failing redress, the chief steward then to report to the Works Committee.

14. The Works Committee shall be empowered to take any case of dispute before the management, not less than three to act as the deputation.

15. On the Works Committee failing to come to any agreement with the management they must immediately report to the Engineering Joint Committee, who shall take up the matter with the firm concerned, a representative of the Works Committee to be one of the deputation. It is essential, pending negotiations, that no stoppage of work shall take place without the sanction of the Engineering Joint Committee.

16. A full list of all shop stewards must be kept by the Joint Committee. Any change of stewards must be reported to the Joint Committee's secretary.

17. The Joint Committee shall be empowered to call meetings of stewards at any works ; also meetings of all chief stewards in the district when the Joint Committee so decides, if necessary.

18. If at any time of dispute the Engineering Joint Committee decides upon withdrawal of its members from any firm or firms, the stewards shall be issued a special official badge from this Committee with the idea of assisting to keep order, if necessary, in the interests of the members concerned.

APPENDIX B

A FIRM'S ' RULES FOR SHOP STEWARDS '

(See Chapter V)

The practice of drawing up rules for shop stewards had hardly been instituted by engineering firms in Great Britain before the war, and was not at any time adopted by the majority of employers. In most cases some degree of ' recognition ' was accorded by the firm without written rules, and frequent disputes arose as to the privileges which recognition involved. The following rules are therefore typical of the practice only of a minority of firms ; but they indicate fairly well the more enlightened type of employers' conception of the province of workshop organization.

REGULATIONS GOVERNING ACTIVITIES OF
SHOP STEWARDS

Meetings.

1. The directors will give the Shop Stewards' Committee facilities for holding committee meetings, including the use of a room, twice per month, one such meeting to take place, unless otherwise arranged, on the first Wednesday of each month at 6.15 p.m.

2. The management will meet the Committee, in general, once per month, such meeting to take place on the second Wednesday at 6.15 p.m. unless otherwise arranged.

3. The directors will allow the Shop Stewards' Committee the use of one of the works dining rooms twice a year, for general works meetings.

4. If extra meetings are desired, either with the management, for

Committee meetings, or for general shop meetings, application should be made to the employment manager.

5. In the case of the regular meetings of the Committee or the monthly joint meetings with the management, if overtime is being worked, and a steward would have been working during a meeting, time spent at such a meeting will be paid for as though spent at work.

Procedure.

6. The superintendent is the executive authority in each department, and his instructions must be obeyed, even though a shop steward considers an order unreasonable. In such a case the constitutional procedure is to obey the order, and to lay a complaint or call for investigation afterwards.

7. Stewards have the right to make any complaint or suggestion to a superintendent with regard to the rules he makes, his treatment of any individual or individuals, his application of general shop rules or policy, &c.

8. In no case will a superintendent refuse to listen to, and investigate, any *bonâ fide* case brought forward by a shop steward, and to give him an answer.

9. If a steward is not satisfied with a superintendent's handling of a question, he may refer the matter to the Shop Stewards' Committee for discussion, if the Committee so desires, with the management at the next monthly joint meeting.

10. It is considered highly desirable that the stewards should get as many questions as possible settled direct with their own superintendents. This does not mean that matters under discussion can be allowed to drag out unnecessarily, and when feeling is running high the shop stewards should take up a question immediately with the employment manager or the works director, but always with the cognisance of the superintendent.

11. When a complaint is made by a steward to a superintendent on behalf of another individual, it must be understood that the superintendent had every right to discuss the matter direct with the individual concerned. This is not intended as a means of putting off the steward, but is a statement of the superintendent's right and duty to maintain the most intimate and friendly relations possible with each and all of his men. In such a case no decision will be come to between the superintendent and the individual except jointly with the steward.

Similarly, every man has a right to approach his superintendent direct, without asking the help of the steward of his department, if he so desires.

General Arrangements and Discipline.

12. The management desires that shop stewards shall have such reasonable facilities as are necessary for carrying out their functions, and expects that in return these will be exercised in such a way as to involve a minimum of interference with their work.

13. Meetings, formal or informal, cannot be held in working hours, except by special permission, and men should not bring grievances or questions to their shop stewards during working hours, but should wait for the next break.

14. Shop stewards may visit the secretary of the Shop Stewards' Committee during working hours on notifying their superintendent. Similarly, the secretary may visit any of the stewards on notifying his superintendent. Each steward is expected to make arrangements mutually satisfactory to his superintendent and himself for the notification of visits when the superintendent is temporarily absent from the department. The time spent in visiting should be restricted as much as possible, and must not be made an excuse for inefficiency of work.

This arrangement is subject to reconsideration, should the number of stewards in the works exceed ten.

15. When decisions are taken at a joint meeting with the management, shop stewards shall not announce same to their men until the dinner-time of the following day, so as to give time for the superintendents to be made cognisant of what transpired.

These regulations are subject to revision at any time by arrangement between the management and the Shop Stewards' Committee.

HANS RENOLD, Ltd.,
Manchester.

20th October, 1917.

APPENDIX C

THE CLYDE WORKERS' COMMITTEE

(See Chapter IX)

The following extracts from the Labour Party Report on the Clyde deportations indicate with some clearness the activities and organization of the most powerful of the Workers' Committees. The student who desires to go further into the subject is strongly recommended to consult the full Report, which was issued separately.

ORIGIN AND DEVELOPMENT

(Extracts from the Report of the Special Committee appointed by the Labour Party to enquire into the Clyde deportations)

The Clyde Workers' Committee was frequently mentioned in the discussion at the Labour Party Conference, and by several of the witnesses in the course of our investigation. We therefore endeavoured to ascertain the origin, constitution, and objects of this organization, but the information we received on the subject was of a somewhat vague and conflicting character. We will endeavour to state briefly what we understand to have been its origin and its position at the time of the strike which resulted in the deportations.

At various times there had been in existence in the Clyde district 'Vigilance Committees', whose primary purpose was active propaganda to persuade non-members to join the Trade Unions. In February 1915, there was a strike, and the Vigilance Committee which then existed, and consisted mainly of shop stewards, added to its numbers and changed its name to that of the ' Labour Withholding Committee ', whose purpose was apparently to act as an unofficial Strike Committee.

Soon after the Munitions Act was passed in July 1915, the ' Labour Withholding Committee ' reconstituted itself as the ' Clyde Workers' Committee ', which met and discussed the Government's arrangements for the dilution of labour, criticized the officials of the Amalgamated Society and other Trade Unions, and discussed a variety of questions affecting workers generally. The President of the Clyde Workers' Committee was Mr. W. Gallacher, the Secretary Mr. J. M. Messer, and the Treasurer Mr. Tom Clark. The Clyde Workers' Committee had neither a constitution nor any rules of a definite character, and although minutes are stated to have been recorded we were informed that no trace of them could be found. It was explained that the Minute Books changed hands and went astray after the deportation of the secretary on the 25th March 1916.

We think the character of the organization can be shown by an extract from the evidence given to us by one of the witnesses :

Q. Were you a member of the Clyde Workers' Committee ?
A. It depends on what you call a member. The Clyde Workers' Committee was a heterogeneous crowd which had practically no constitution. It was more a collection of angry Trade Unionists than anything else, which had sprung into existence because of the trouble which was going on on the Clyde. The Clyde Workers' Committee was the result of the trouble, the outcome of the trouble. It was a place of meeting where the different kindred spirits of the different shops met to discuss all our grievances.
Q. Did you think it better to go there than to go to your own Trade Union officials ?

A. Oh, yes. Our own Trade Union officials were hopelessly tied up, and if you spoke to them, they were tied up. They could do nothing.

Q. They were tied up by whom ?

A. Under the Munitions Act.

Q. Accepted by the Amalgamated Society of Engineers ?

A. The Munitions Act ?

Q. Yes.

A. I understood it was accepted by all the Trade Unions. I never knew of an official strike taking place under the Munitions Act.

Q. Do you think the establishment of a Committee such as the Clyde Workers' Committee was likely to help the Trade Union movement, or the reverse ?

A. I do not know. It welded together the men in the workshops who felt they had grievances.

Q. But would it not be disintegrating, rather than unifying, and probably lead to a new breakaway, to a new Union : was not that the tendency ?

A. Not necessarily, because if you take the membership of the Clyde Workers' Committee, when the men in the workshop agreed to affiliate to the Clyde Workers' Committee, they usually sent their shop stewards as their representatives, so that, as a matter of fact, being a shop steward was one of the qualifications for being the representative of the Committee. Where they previously had sent their shop stewards to the Society to report to their District Committee, the shop stewards were sent to the Clyde Workers' Committee.

Q. You do not know whether you are a member ?

A. I was the representative from the Diesel.

Q. You do not know exactly whether you are a member. There was a certain number of these who acted as an Executive, there was a secretary and there was a president ?

A. Yes.

Q. Who appointed them ?

A. Those shop stewards who attended, but you must remember that it was not absolutely necessary for your shop to send you ; you could represent a minority in the shop just the same as a majority, even though the minority was one.

Q. Could you represent yourself alone ?

A. You could. I did not ; I represented the shop.

Q. Therefore it was not a democratic constitution, at any rate ?

A. I do not know about it not being a very democratic constitution. I would hardly care to say that. If you went there you could only speak for yourself if you were only representing yourself, but if you represented the department you could speak for the department.

The foregoing and other similar evidence indicates that membership of the Clyde Workers' Committee was of the loosest possible description. Funds were raised by voluntary subscriptions in the works. In our view, the members did not give sufficiently serious consideration to the probable ultimate consequences of some of the lines of policy advocated and approved at their meetings; in fact irresponsibility appears to have been one of. the characteristics of the organization.

Soon after the Munitions of War Act was passed in July, 1915, the Clyde Workers' Committee issued the following manifesto :

CLYDE WORKERS' COMMITTEE

ʼThe support given to the Munitions Act by the officials was an act of treachery to the working classes. Those of us who refused to be sold have organized the above Committee representative of all trades in the Clyde area, determined to retain what liberties we have, and to take the first opportunity of forcing the repeal of all the pernicious legislation that has recently been imposed upon us. In the words of a manifesto issued by the Trade Union Rights Committee, recently formed in London :

> Let us preserve what rights still remain and refuse steadfastly to surrender another inch to our allied foes—the capitalists and politicians. The liberty and freedom of the organized worker is the one thing; our fight is the fight that matters and now is the time to act.

It is composed of delegates of shop stewards from all trades in the Glasgow area, and is open to all such bona fide workers. The progressives in all trades are invited to attend. Its origin goes back to the last big strike of February, 1915, when action was taken to force the demand put forward for an increase of 2d. per hour in the engineering industry. At that time a Committee known as the Labour Withholding Committee was set up, representative of the different trades in the industry, to organize the strike, and notwithstanding the fierce opposition from public opinion, employers, Government, and our own officials alike, that Committee managed and carried through probably the best-organized strike in the annals of Clyde history, and brought about closer working unity amongst the rank and file of the different trades than years of official effort. It became obvious then that such a Committee permanently established would be invaluable to the workers, and with that purpose in view the Committee was kept in being after the termination of the strike.

Our purpose must not be misconstrued. We are out for unity and closer organization of all trades in the industry, one Union being the ultimate aim. We will support the officials just so long as they rightly represent the workers, but we will act independently immediately they misrepresent them. Being composed of delegates from every shop and untrammelled by obsolete rule or law, we claim to represent the true feeling of the workers. We can act immediately according to the merits of the case and the desires of the rank and file.

Signed on behalf of the Committee,
WM. GALLACHER, President.
J. M. MESSER, Secretary.
408, Allison Street.

The evidence shows that this manifesto was approved, signed, and issued without due consideration having been given to it and without any sense of responsibility for the very arbitrary statements which it contained.

On the 8th January 1916 the Clyde Workers' Committee appears to have started a weekly paper under the title of *The Worker*, but its fourth and final issue was suppressed towards the end of the month.[1]

NEW METHODS OF WORKSHOP CONTROL ADVOCATED BY THE CLYDE WORKERS' COMMITTEE

The Clyde Workers' Committee advocated the view that the organized Trade Unionists should be allowed to share in the administration and control of workshop arrangements, more particularly in munitions factories which had been brought under the control of the Government, but its witnesses emphatically denied having stipulated on the occasion of Mr. Lloyd George's visit to the Clyde district in December, 1915, that dilution would not be agreed to unless the munitions works were handed over to their sole control. On the other hand, both Mr. Henderson and Mr. Lynden Macassey, who were present at all Mr. Lloyd George's meetings, stated quite definitely that claims of that absolute character were made by members of the Clyde Workers' Committee.

We find that in a copy of *The Worker*, the organ of the Clyde Workers' Committee, for the 8th January 1916, in an article entitled ' Our Case in Brief,' Mr. J. W. Muir, who apparently edited the paper, stated in regard to the policy of the Clyde Workers' Committee : 'the Government must take over all the industries and national resources and give organized labour a direct share in the management down through all the departments.' In another part of the paper containing a report of the meeting of the shop stewards at Parkhead Forge, which was addressed by Mr. Lloyd George, it was stated :

> When he finished, Kirkwood asked if he was prepared to give the workers a share in the management of the works. They as Socialists welcomed dilution of labour which they regarded as the natural development in industrial conditions. They were not like the Luddites of another generation who smashed the new machinery. But this scheme of dilution must be carried out under the control of the workers. They recognized that if they had not control, cheap labour would be introduced, and unless their demand was granted they would fight the scheme to the death.

It will be observed that, according to the report in *The Worker*,

---

[1] This paper was reissued later, and now appears as the organ of the Workers' Committee Movement.

Mr. Muir (who, like Mr. Kirkwood, belonged to the Amalgamated Society of Engineers, and was a very active member of the Clyde Workers' Committee), and also Mr. Kirkwood, claimed only a *share* in the management of the workshops, and that Mr. Kirkwood was apparently apprehensive that unless the scheme of dilution was carried out under the control of the workers it would be exploited by the introduction of cheap labour. Seeing that it was proposed to bring in large numbers of unskilled workers, including women, this apprehension was very natural on the part of the skilled engineers whose province would thus be invaded.

In this connection we might mention that Messrs. Wm. Beardmore & Co., Ltd., had strongly opposed the Amalgamated Society some years previously, and had only made their place a ' Union shop ' about three months after the commencement of the war. It is quite conceivable that during the excitement and the somewhat heated discussions which arose at some of Mr. Lloyd George's meetings in the Clyde district in December, 1915, some of the speakers put up what was literally an unqualified claim to complete control of the workshops ; but so far as we could ascertain, the intention of the leading members of the Clyde Workers' Committee was that the system of control should be operated through the Trade Unions in conjunction with the Government and the management in the various works.

THE CLYDE WORKERS' COMMITTEE AND ITS STRIKE POLICY

We interrogated the representatives of the Clyde Workers' Committee with regard to the general question of strikes and the alleged responsibility of that Committee for the strike which resulted in the deportations. They stated most definitely that the Committee did not exist to promote strikes, and that its chairman had publicly announced on more than one occasion prior to the strike which preceded the deportations that the Clyde Workers' Committee had no power to declare a strike. They further maintained that they were not responsible for that particular strike, and asserted that the Committee was more of an educative and propagandist body than anything else ; that it strongly advocated Industrial Unionism in preference to Sectional or Craft Unionism, and that it existed to watch and discuss matters of general interest to workers, especially in regard to the exceptional conditions which arose out of the war.

In spite of these assertions of the witnesses who represented the Clyde Workers' Committee, that it did not exist to promote strikes, the contrary spirit was apparent in its weekly paper *The Worker* ; and the manifesto issued soon after the passing of the Munitions of

War Act in July, 1915, claimed that the Committee under its previous title had ' managed and carried through probably the best organized strike in the annals of Clyde history.'

However, we do not think that the Clyde Workers' Committee as a collective body was responsible for starting the strike which occurred at Parkhead Forge in March, 1916. In our opinion, that strike was a spontaneous outbreak of the general body of workmen employed there, and was intended as a protest against what they regarded as the unfair restriction of facilities which had previously been allowed to the chief shop steward.

APPENDIX D

THE WORKERS' COMMITTEE

(See Chapter X)

The pamphlet from which these extracts are taken is fully dealt with in Chapter X of the text. It describes, not the actual achievements of the Workers' Committee movement, but the aspirations of one of its leaders, Mr. J. T. Murphy of Sheffield. It should not be assumed that the movement as a whole necessarily endorsed Mr. Murphy's ideas, although they are fairly typical of the general aims of the left-wing sections.

Extracts from Mr. J. T. Murphy's pamphlet, *The Workers' Committee*, published in 1918 by the Sheffield Workers' Committee.

THE WORKSHOP COMMITTEE

The procedure to adopt is to form in every workshop a Workshop Committee, composed of shop stewards, elected by the workers in the workshops. Skilled, semi-skilled, and unskilled workers should all have their shop stewards, and due regard be given also to the particular union to which each worker belongs.

For example : Suppose a workshop is composed of members of the General Labourers' Union, Workers' Union, A.S.E., Steam Engine Makers, Women Workers, &c., each of these unions should have their shop stewards, and the whole co-operate together, and form the Workshop Committee.

Immediately this will stimulate the campaign for the elimination of the non-unionist. We know of one shop where, as soon as the Workshop Committee was formed, every union benefited in membership, and one Society enrolled sixty members.

Where possible, it is advisable for shop stewards to be officially

recognized, and to be supplied with rules which lend support and
encourage the close co-operation which a Workshop Committee requires.

We suggest the following as a shop steward's instruction card, for
any of the Societies :

Members' pence cards should be inspected every six weeks.

New arrivals into workshops shall be approached by the shop
steward nearest to such and questioned as to membership of
a trade union.

Steward shall demand the production of pence card of alleged
member.

Steward shall take note of shop conditions, wages, &c., in the area
in which he is acting as shop steward, and report any violations
of district conditions as approved by the trade unions which
are not immediately remedied to the trade union officials.

Any dispute arising between employer and employee, which results
in a challenge of district conditions as approved, shall be
reported to the shop steward.

Steward shall then consult with other shop stewards as to the
course of procedure to be adopted, the results of such consultation to be submitted to the members in the shop for approval.

Matters which affect more than one department shall be dealt
with in a similar manner by the stewards in the affected areas.

The workers in the workshop should attempt to remedy their
grievances in the workshop before calling in official aid.

Where members of other unions are affected, their co-operation
should be sought.

We would also advise that there be one shop steward to not more
than fifteen workers.   The more active workers there are the better and
easier is the organizing work carried on.   Also elect a convener in each
shop for each class of worker.   Their duties will be to call shop stewards'
meetings in the shop, and be delegates to the district meetings.   Other
duties we shall mention later.

The initiative should be taken by the workers in the various districts.
It is immaterial whether the first move is made through the local
trade union committees, or in the workshops and then through the
committee, so long as the stewards are elected in the workshops and
not in the branches.   The means are then assured of an alliance between
official and unofficial activities by an official recognition of rank and
file control.

Having now described how the workshop committees can be formed,
and how the committees can be at the same time part of the official
trade union movement, we must now proceed to show how the movement
can grow, and how it must grow to meet the demands of the day.

LOCAL INDUSTRIAL COMMITTEES

should be formed in each district.   It will be readily perceived that
no one firm will be completely organized before the workers in other
firms begin to move in the same direction.   Therefore in the early stages
of development, full shop stewards' meetings should be held in every

district, and an Industrial Administrative Committee be formed from these meetings. The size of the committee will vary according to the size of the district, so we will leave that to the discretion of those who form the committee. The functions of these committees are mainly those of educating and co-ordinating the efforts of the rank and file through the shop stewards. For example—one committee provides information relative to agreed upon district conditions, Munitions Act, Military Service agreement, Labour Advisory Board, Procedure in the workshops, &c. Then this committee should be the means of extending and developing the organizations, so that the workers can obtain the maximum of power in their hands.

The committee should not usurp the functions of the local trade union committees, but attend to the larger questions, embracing all the trade unions in the industry.

It will have been observed that we have addressed ourselves, so far as practical procedure is concerned, to the Engineering workers. This we have done because the nucleus of the larger organization has already come into being through that industry, and presents us with a clear line of development. So far, then, we have shown how to form a Workshop Committee, and an Engineering Workers' Committee in a locality. These committees should not have any governing power, but should exist to render service to the rank and file, by providing means for them to arrive at decisions and to unite their forces.

WORKS OR PLANT COMMITTEES

The next step is to intensify the development of the workshop committees by the formation on every plant of a Plant Committee. To achieve this all the stewards of each firm, from every department of that firm, should meet and elect a committee from amongst them to centralize the efforts or link up the shop committees in the firm. The need for this development we will endeavour to make clear. Just as it is necessary to co-operate the workshops for production, so it is necessary to co-ordinate the work of the shop committees. As there are questions which affect a single department, so there are questions which affect the plant as a whole. The function of a Plant Committee will be such that every question, every activity, can be known throughout the departments at the earliest possible moment, and the maximum of attention be rapidly developed. The complaints of workers that they do not know what is happening would become less frequent. The trick of ' playing ' one department against another to cut rates could easily be stopped, and so on.

APPENDIX E

THE WHITLEY REPORT ON WORKS COMMITTEES

(See Chapter XIII)

The Whitley Committee, or, to give its official name, the Ministry of Reconstruction Committee on the Relations between Employers and Employed, was the body responsible for the Whitley Report, under which Standing Joint Industrial Councils were established, with Government endorsement, by Employers' Associations and Trade Unions in a number of industries. An integral part of the scheme propounded by the Committee was that not only National and District Industrial Councils, but also Works Committees, should be established. This, however, only took place in a very few cases (see Chapter XIII). The following Report is supplementary to the main Whitley Report on Joint Industrial Councils.

SUPPLEMENTARY REPORT ON WORKS COMMITTEES [1]

To the Right Honourable D. LLOYD GEORGE, M.P., Prime Minister.

SIR,

In our first and second Reports we have referred to the establishment of Works Committees,[2] representative of the management and of the workpeople, and appointed from within the works, as an essential part of the scheme of organization suggested to secure improved relations between employers and employed. The purpose of the present Report is to deal more fully with the proposal to institute such Committees.

2. Better relations between employers and their workpeople can best be arrived at by granting to the latter a greater share in the consideration of matters with which they are concerned. In every industry there are certain questions, such as rates of wages and hours of work, which should be settled by District or National agreement, and with any matter so settled no Works Committee should be allowed to inter-

---

[1] Reprinted, by permission of the Controller of H.M. Stationery Office, from the Ministry of Reconstruction's ' Supplementary Report on Works Committees, Cd. 9001 ', 1918.

[2] In the use of the term ' Works Committees ' in this Report it is not intended to use the word ' works ' in a technical sense ; in such an industry as the Coal Trade, for example, the ' Pit Committees ' would probably be the term used in adopting the scheme.

fere ; but there are also many questions closely affecting daily life and
comfort in, and the success of, the business, and affecting in no small
degree efficiency of working, which are peculiar to the individual
workshop or factory. The purpose of a Works Committee is to establish
and maintain a system of co-operation in all these workshop matters.

3. We have throughout our recommendations proceeded upon the
assumption that the greatest success is likely to be achieved by leaving
to the representative bodies of employers and employed in each industry
the maximum degree of freedom to settle for themselves the precise form
of Council or Committee which should be adopted, having regard in
each case to the particular circumstances of the trade ; and in accordance with this principle, we refrain from indicating any definite form
of constitution for the Works Committees. Our proposals as a whole
assume the existence of organizations of both employers and employed
and a frank and full recognition of such organizations. Works Committees established otherwise than in accordance with these principles
could not be regarded as part of the scheme we have recommended,
and might indeed be a hindrance to the development of the new relations
in industry to which we look forward. We think the aim should be the
complete and coherent organization of the trade on both sides, and
Works Committees will be of value in so far as they contribute to such
a result.

4. We are of opinion that the complete success of Works Committees
necessarily depends largely upon the degree and efficiency of organization
in the trade, and upon the extent to which the Committees can be
linked up, through organizations that we have in mind, with the remainder of the scheme which we are proposing, viz. the District and
National Councils. We think it important to state that the success of
the Works Committees would be very seriously interfered with if the
idea existed that such Committees were used, or likely to be used, by
employers in opposition to Trade Unionism. It is strongly felt that
the setting up of Works Committees without the co-operation of the
Trade Unions and the Employers' Associations in the trade or branch
of trade concerned would stand in the way of the improved industrial
relationships which in these Reports we are endeavouring to further.

5. In an industry where the workpeople are unorganized, or only
very partially organized, there is a danger that Works Committees may
be used, or thought to be used, in opposition to Trade Unionism. It
is important that such fears should be guarded against in the initiation
of any scheme. We look upon successful Works Committees as the
broad base of the Industrial Structure which we have recommended,
and as the means of enlisting the interest of the workers in the success
both of the industry to which they are attached and of the workshop or
factory where so much of their life is spent. These Committees should

not, in constitution or methods of working, discourage Trade organizations.

6. Works Committees, in our opinion, should have regular meetings at fixed times, and, as a general rule, not less frequently than once a fortnight. They should always keep in the forefront the idea of constructive co-operation in the improvement of the industry to which they belong. Suggestions of all kinds tending to improvement should be frankly welcomed and freely discussed. Practical proposals should be examined from all points of view. There is an undeveloped asset of constructive ability—valuable alike to the industry and to the State—awaiting the means of realization ; problems, old and new, will find their solution in a frank partnership of knowledge, experience and goodwill. Works Committees would fail in their main purpose if they existed only to smooth over grievances.

7. We recognize that, from time to time, matters will arise which the management or the workmen consider to be questions they cannot discuss in these joint meetings. When this occurs, we anticipate that nothing but good will come from the friendly statement of the reasons why the reservation is made.

8. We regard the successful development and utilization of Works Committees in any business on the basis recommended in this Report as of equal importance with its commercial and scientific efficiency ; and we think that in any case one of the partners or directors, or some other responsible representative of the management, would be well advised to devote a substantial part of his time and thought to the good working and development of such a committee.

9. There has been some experience, both before the war and during the war, of the benefits of Works Committees, and we think it should be recommended most strongly to employers and employed that, in connection with the scheme for the establishment of National and District Industrial Councils, they should examine this experience with a view to the institution of Works Committees on proper lines, in works where the conditions render their formation practicable. We have recommended that the Ministry of Labour should prepare a summary of the experience available with reference to Works Committees, both before and during the war, including information as to any rules or reports relating to such Committees, and should issue a memorandum thereon for the guidance of employers and workpeople generally, and we understand that such a memorandum is now in course of preparation.

10. In order to ensure uniform and common principles of action, it is essential that where National and District Industrial Councils exist the Works Committees should be in close touch with them, and the scheme for linking up Works Committees with the Councils should be considered and determined by the National Councils.

11. We have considered it better not to attempt to indicate any specific form of Works Committees. Industrial establishments show such infinite variation in size, number of persons employed, multiplicity of departments, and other conditions, that the particular form of Works Committees must necessarily be adapted to the circumstances of each case. It would, therefore, be impossible to formulate any satisfactory scheme which does not provide a large measure of elasticity.

We are confident that the nature of the particular organization necessary for the various cases will be settled without difficulty by the exercise of goodwill on both sides.

We have the honour to be,

Sir,

Your obedient Servants,[1]

J. H. WHITLEY, *Chairman.*

F. S. BUTTON.

S. J. CHAPMAN.

G. H. CLAUGHTON.

J. R. CLYNES.

F. N. HEPWORTH.

WILFRID HILL.

J. A. HOBSON.

A. SUSAN LAWRENCE.

MAURICE LEVY.

J. J. MALLON.

THOS. R. RATCLIFFE-ELLIS.

ALLAN M. SMITH.

D. R. H. WILLIAMS.

MONA WILSON.

H. J. WILSON,   } *Secretaries.*
A. GREENWOOD, }

18*th October*, 1917.

---

[1] Sir G. J. Carter and Mr. Smillie were unable to attend any of the meetings at which this Report was considered, and they therefore do not sign it. Sir G. J. Carter has intimated that in his view, in accordance with the principles indicated in paragraphs 3, 4, and 5 of the Report, it is important that Works Committees should not deal with matters which ought to be directly dealt with by the firms concerned or their respective Associations in conjunction with the recognized representatives of the Trade Unions whose members are affected.

APPENDIX F

THE MINISTRY OF LABOUR'S 'NOTES ON WORKS COMMITTEES' UNDER THE WHITLEY SCHEME

(See Chapter XIII)

The following 'Notes on Works Committees'[1] were drawn up, not by the Whitley Committee, which was responsible for the Report printed in Appendix E, but by the Ministry of Labour. The Ministry, on the acceptance of the Whitley scheme by the Government, was charged with its administration, and held a watching brief in all negotiations for the formation of Joint Industrial Councils. The Ministry, however, while it could withhold approval from any scheme, had no power to determine its provisions. These 'Notes' are therefore merely recommendations, and possess no binding character.

III. WORKS COMMITTEES

Suggestions prepared by the Ministry of Labour as to the Constitution and Functions of Works Committees in industries in which National Joint Industrial Councils are established.

The differing circumstances of different industries make it impossible to devise any scheme suitable to every industry. Again, the type of Works Committee suitable will vary with the size of the firm and the form taken by organization among the employees. In preparing a scheme, therefore, the machinery outlined in the following suggestions may require to be adapted in greater or lesser degree if the general objects for which Works Committees are recommended are to be attained. At the same time, anything that is done—whether or not it is embodied in the Works Rules drawn up by the Works Committee—must be consistent with the principles of the collective agreements accepted by the District and National Authorities. For this reason steps should be taken to secure the closest possible connection between the Works Committee and the District and National Councils.

OBJECTS

1. The object of the Works Committee is to provide a recognized means of consultation between the management and the employees, and

---

[1] Reprinted by permission of the Controller of H.M. Stationery Office, from the Ministry of Labour's 'Notes on Works Committees under the Whitley Scheme'.

(i) to give the employees a wider interest in and greater responsibility for the conditions under which their work is performed,

(ii) to enforce the regulations contained in collective agreements drawn up by District and National Authorities,

(iii) to prevent friction and misunderstanding.

FUNCTIONS

2. Matters to be dealt with by the Works Committee shall include :

(This list of functions is not meant to be exhaustive. Almost every industry has rules or customs which arise from the particular conditions under which the work of the industry is carried on (e. g., the payment of ' dirty money,' provision of tools, allowances for working away from the works or from home, allowances on standard district piece prices for deficiences in material or machinery, &c.). In a well-regulated industry many such matters will be subject to district or national agreements, and the powers of a Works Committee will be limited in the same manner as they will be in regard to the more general questions of district or national agreement (standard rates, piece prices, normal hours, overtime, &c.). No attempt has been made to include such questions as arise only in some industries, for which each National Council concerned will have to decide upon a method of regulation, including the powers to be vested in Works Committees.)

(a) The issue and revision of works rules.

(b) The distribution of working hours ; breaks ; time recording, &c.

(c) The method of payment of wages (time, form of pay ticket, &c.) ; explanation of methods of payment ; the adjustment of piece prices, subject to district or national agreements ; records of piece prices ; deductions, &c.

(d) The settlement of grievances.

(e) Holiday arrangements.

(f) Questions of physical welfare (provision of meals, drinking water, lavatories and washing accommodation, cloakrooms, ventilation, heating, lighting and sanitation ; accidents, safety appliances, first aid, ambulance, &c.).

(g) Questions of discipline and conduct as between management and workpeople (malingering ; bullying ; time keeping ; publicity in regard to rules ; supervision of notice boards, &c.).

(h) Terms of engagement of workpeople.

(i) The training of apprentices and young persons.

(j) Technical library ; lectures on the technical and social aspects of the industry.

(k) Suggestions of improvements in method and organization of work ; the testing of suggestions.

(l) Investigation of circumstances tending to reduce efficiency or in any way to interfere with the satisfactory working of the factory.

(*m*) Collections (for clubs, charities, &c.).

(*n*) Entertainments and sports.

(*o*) The provision of facilities for the employees' side of the Joint Committee (or of a departmental committee, if any) to conduct its own work.

(It may be found necessary to leave certain questions to be settled not by the whole Works Committee, but by a sub-committee of it on which the workers' representatives are drawn only from the particular department or section directly concerned, for example, a piecework question in one department of a works which is mainly on timework. The size of the works, also, is a factor which must be taken into account in considering the need for sub-committees. In some instances departmental sub-committees and in others functional sub-committees (e. g. a 'Safety' Committee or a Welfare Committee) may best suit the circumstances. Even where definite sub-committees are not arranged for, work of the same kind as these would perform may often be carried out by consultation between the representatives of the management and the secretary of the workers' side, along with the representatives of a department.)

3. The Works Committee shall not have any power to come to an agreement inconsistent with the powers or decisions of the District or National Councils or with any agreement between a trade union and the employers' association. Further, any agreement come to by a Works Committee may at any time be superseded by the District or National Council or by agreement between a trade union and the employers' association.

CONSTITUTION

4. The Works Committee shall consist of   members, of whom shall represent the management and   shall represent the employees.

(To have an equal number of members on the two sides would in most works be impracticable, and, in view of the suggested procedure, is unnecessary. The number required on the management side will vary, but 2, 3 or 4 is suggested as a suitable number. The number of employees' representatives will vary with the size and complexity of the particular works. Some number from 5 to 12 is suggested as likely to suit most circumstances.)

5. Either side shall have the right to add to its numbers representatives of the particular departments or sections of departments affected by a question under discussion and not directly represented on the Committee. The addition shall be made only for the period

during which the question affecting the particular departments or sections of departments is before the Committee.

6. The representatives of the management on the Committee shall be appointed by the firm.

(*Certain members of the managerial staff should form a constant nucleus of the management side. This nucleus should be made up of such individuals as a Managing Director, the Works Manager, and, where there is such an official, the Labour or Welfare Superintendent.*)

7. The employees' side of the Works Committee shall be Trade Union members, elected as hereinafter provided.

(*The National and District Councils are based solely upon the representation of organizations. In the case of the works, in order to secure cohesion of policy as between the Works Committee and the District and National Councils, it is advisable that the Works Committee should normally be based on a recognition of the workpeople's organizations. But, in particular factories where the employees are not strongly organized, or where the functions of the Works Committee are such as to require the presence of workers who are not organized, it may be found necessary to depart from the principle laid down above. In these circumstances, however, the shop stewards, or other trade union representatives in the works, should be consulted on all questions affecting district or national agreements. Any deviation from the general scheme should be adopted only after approval by the Industrial Council on a consideration of the merits of the case.*)

8. Employee members shall hold office for a period of 12 months ending on the   day of   in each year. On any representative leaving the employment of the firm or resigning his position as member, a successor shall be appointed in the ordinary way by the department or section concerned, to hold office for the remainder of the term.

ELECTIONS

9. Elections of employees' representatives on the Works Committee shall be held in the month of   in each year.

(*Each works should draw up a scheme of constituencies and a method of election to suit its own particular conditions. It is suggested that a provisional committee should be appointed for this purpose. The representation should normally be on the basis of departments, due allowance being made for the various sections of workers engaged in any department. In order that this may not sometimes necessitate a Committee of unwieldy size, it is suggested that for large or complex works the employees' side of the Joint Committee should be appointed by and from a larger body of workers' representatives elected from the various departments. In large works it will probably be found desirable to establish departmental committees, with a Works Committee representative of all the departments chosen from the departmental committees. In such cases the functions of the departmental committees will be confined to matters affecting the department only, whilst the Works Committee will consider questions affecting more than one department or the whole works. The workers' side of a departmental committee should be so elected as to give representation to each of the various sections of workers engaged in the department.)*

10. The election should be by ballot, or by departmental or sectional meetings specially convened for the purpose.

11. A serving member of the Committee shall be eligible for re-election.

OFFICERS

12. The Works Committee shall appoint a Chairman and a Vice-Chairman from the two sides respectively. Each side shall appoint its own Secretary.

PROCEDURE

13. Meetings of the Works Committee shall be held at regular intervals of $\frac{\text{(two)}}{\text{(four)}}$ weeks. The meetings shall be held during working hours.

14. Special meetings of the Works Committee shall be called at hours' notice on a request on behalf of one side by its secretary to the secretary of the other side.

15. The agenda of business shall be submitted by the secretaries to each member of the Committee at least   hours before a meeting, except in the case of special meetings.

16. No business other than that appearing on the agenda shall be transacted at any meeting unless both sides agree to its introduction.

17. When an individual employee desires to bring any question before the Committee, he or she should report to his or her departmental or sectional representative, who in the case of grievances shall endeavour to reach a settlement. Failing a settlement, the representative shall inform the employees' secretary. The latter shall endeavour to arrange a settlement. Failing a settlement, the question shall come before the Works Committee.

18. In the course of his duties the secretary of the employees' side should have the right to enter any department in the works, and the representative of any department or section the right to enter the department in which the secretary is at work.

19. Facilities should be provided for meetings of the employees' side of the Committee in the works, normally after working hours or during meal hours.

20. The workers' representatives should be paid at their ordinary rate for time spent at meetings of the Works Committee.

21. Duplicate books of minutes should be kept, one by the secretary of each side.

22. Copies of the minutes of all meetings of the Works Committee must be sent to the secretaries of the District Council within 7 days of the date of meeting.

23. Decisions shall be arrived at only by agreement between the two sides.

24. The presence of   members from each side of the Committee shall be necessary to form a quorum.

25. In the event of any matter arising which the Committee cannot agree upon, the officials of the trade union or unions concerned shall negotiate with the firm, or, if desired, with the officials of the employers' association. The question may thereafter be referred by either side to the District Council.

26. The recognized district official of any trade union or employers' association concerned may attend any meeting in an advisory capacity.

ALTHOUGH THE ABOVE SUGGESTIONS HAVE BEEN PREPARED AS A GUIDE IN FRAMING A CONSTITUTION FOR A WORKS COMMITTEE IT IS RECOGNIZED THAT THE DETAILS OF SUCH A CONSTITUTION MUST VARY TO MEET THE CONDITIONS AND REQUIREMENTS OF PARTICULAR WORKS. THE ASSISTANCE OF OFFICERS OF THE MINISTRY OF LABOUR WITH EXPERIENCE OF WORKS COMMITTEES IS AVAILABLE IN CONNECTION WITH THE DRAFTING OF CONSTITUTIONS AND THE SETTING UP OF WORKS COMMITTEES.

APPENDIX G

THE WHITLEY SCHEME IN THE ROYAL DOCKYARDS

(See Chapter XIII)

The application of the Whitley scheme to the Government's own employees presented special problems. The following constitution shows how it was put into operation in the largest group of Government establishments apart from the Post Office. It was also applied to the Post Office and to the administrative departments of the Civil Service, but a study of its application in these cases falls outside the scope of a study dealing with ' Workshop Organization '.

APPLICATION OF THE WHITLEY REPORT TO GOVERNMENT INDUSTRIAL ESTABLISHMENTS

ADMIRALTY DEPARTMENTAL JOINT COUNCIL

CONSTITUTION

(Adopted at the First Meeting of the Council,
10th October, 1919.)

OBJECTS.

1. *General Object.* To secure, by means of regular joint discussion between official representatives of the Admiralty and representatives of the Trade Unions having members employed in the industrial establishments of the department, the fullest measure of co-operation in their administration and work in the national interests, and with a view to the increased well-being of all employed therein.

It will be open to the Council to consider any matters that fall within the scope of this general definition except such as are specifically reserved as the exclusive functions of a Trade Joint Council. Among its more specific objects will be the following :

2. Regular consideration of working conditions in the department's industrial establishments.

3. The consideration of measures for regularizing production and employment.

4. The consideration of the methods by which the above objects can best be secured, and of local and other machinery for the settlement of differences between different parties in the various establishments, with the object of securing the speedy settlement of difficulties.

5. The collection, as required, of statistics and information on matters relevant to the work of the various establishments.

6. The consideration of the best means of securing the highest efficiency of the department's establishments, including inventions, and any improvements in machinery, methods or organization by which this can be attained ; to secure that such inventions or improvements shall give to each party a fair distribution of the benefits derived from the increased efficiency ; the utilization to the fullest extent of the practical knowledge and experience of the workpeople, and the creation of facilities for such knowledge to receive adequate consideration.

7. The maintenance of a high standard of health among the workers in the various establishments, and the consideration of problems relating to welfare, industrial fatigue, factory and workshop equipment, &c., in their relation to health and efficiency.

8. The consideration of the conditions of entry into, and training

in the various establishments concerned, in conjunction with the Trade Joint Councils where necessary, and of educational questions in relation thereto.

9. The consideration of matters of a general nature such as sick absence, holidays, retirement and superannuation.

10. The consideration of arrangements for setting up and adjusting local machinery by way of works, shop or other committees, to deal with any or all of the above matters, and the consideration of matters referred to the Council by such committees.

11. Co-operation with other Departmental Joint Councils or with Joint Industrial Councils in private industry, where necessary, to deal with matters of common interest.

CONSTITUTION

1. MEMBERSHIP

The Council shall consist of 24 members appointed as to the official side by the Admiralty, except as to one representative appointed by the Minister of Labour, and as to the employees' side by the Trade Unions having members employed in the various establishments.

No. of Representatives.

Official Side :

Admiralty	8
Ministry of Labour	1
Total	9

Employees' Side : Groups of Trade Unions :

Engineering and Shipbuilding	7
Building.	2
Miscellaneous	1
General Labour	5
Total	15

Provided that so far as the departments and the Trade Unions consider necessary, adequate provision is made by the constituent bodies for the appointment of persons directly connected with the various establishments under the department. It shall be open, however, with the permission of the Council, for a national or local representative of any constituent body, other than a member of the Council, to attend a meeting in a consultative capacity.

Provided also that at any time after the expiration of six months from the date of the first meeting of the Council, on the request, of which one calendar month's notice shall be given, of the Admiralty or of any constituent Trade Union on the employees' side, a General Meeting of the Council may be convened to consider and approve the redistribution of the nominations amongst the constituent bodies, provided however, that one side can call only for a revision of its own representatives.

Representation of the Treasury. Ordinarily the Treasury will not be represented upon a Departmental Joint Council, but when any item appears upon the Agenda which in the opinion of the Chairman involves an important matter for the consideration of the Treasury, he shall make arrangements for that Department to be represented at the meeting of the Council.

Provided also that when giving notice of a motion it shall be open to a member on the employees' side to request the Chairman to arrange for the attendance of a Treasury representative.

2. RE-APPOINTMENT

The representatives first appointed shall serve for one year from the date of the first meeting, and shall be eligible for re-appointment by the Admiralty (or Minister of Labour), or Trade Unions as the case may be. Casual vacancies shall be filled as they occur in the same manner as the original appointment, the member so appointed sitting for the remainder of the current term of the Council.

Provided, however, that where a representative cannot attend a meeting of the Council, an accredited deputy may be sent by the Admiralty (or Minister of Labour) or the Trade Union concerned.

3. COMMITTEES

The Council may delegate special powers to any committee it appoints. It may appoint an Executive Committee, and such other Standing, Section or other committees as may be necessary. The reports of all committees shall be submitted to the Council for confirmation.

The Council shall have power to appoint on committees, other than the Executive Committee, such persons not necessarily being members of the Council as may serve the special purposes of the Council.

4. CO-OPTED MEMBERS

The Council may allow committees, other than the Executive Committee, to co-opt such persons of special knowledge, not being members of the Council, as may serve the special purposes of theCouncil.

5. OFFICERS

Chairman.—The Chairman shall be a member of the Council appointed by the Admiralty.

The *Vice-Chairman* shall be a member appointed by the employees' side of the Council and shall preside at meetings in the absence of the Chairman. In the absence of both the Chairman and the Vice-Chairman, a Chairman shall be appointed by and from the members present at the meeting.

Secretaries.—A Secretary shall be appointed from each side of the Council. The necessary clerical assistance required at meetings of the Council shall be provided by the Department.

6. MEETINGS OF THE COUNCIL

The ordinary meetings of the Council shall be held as often as necessary, and not less than once a quarter. The meeting in the month of October shall be the annual meeting. An agenda shall be circulated to all members not less than seven days prior to the meeting of the Council.

A special meeting of the Council shall be called within 14 days by either secretary on the receipt of a requisition from the secretary of the other side. The matters to be discussed at a special meeting shall be stated upon the notice summoning the meeting.

7. VOTING

Decisions of the Council shall normally be by agreement, but a vote may be taken by a show of hands or otherwise as may be determined. No resolution shall be regarded as carried unless it has been approved by a majority of the members present on each side of the Council.

8. QUORUM

The quorum shall be a majority of the members of each side of the Council.

9. EXPENSES

The Trade Unions or groups of Trade Unions shall be responsible for the travelling and other personal expenses of their representatives attending meetings of the Council or its Committees.

10. AMENDMENT OF CONSTITUTION

The ' Objects and Constitution ' of the Council may be amended at the Annual General Meeting, or at an Extra-ordinary General Meeting of the Council. No amendment shall be made except after notice given and circulated on the agenda to the members of the Council at least fourteen days prior to the meeting.

THE WHITLEY SCHEME IN THE ROYAL DOCKYARDS

CONSTITUTION AND FUNCTIONS OF SHOP, DEPARTMENT AND YARD COMMITTEES IN ADMIRALTY INDUSTRIAL ESTABLISHMENTS.

1. The broad object for which these Committees are constituted is to provide a recognized means of consultation between the management and the employees in the respective establishments and :

(1) to provide that the employees are given a wider interest in, and greater responsibility for, the conditions under which their work is performed.

(2) that the regulations contained in collective agreements made in the Departmental and Trade Joint Councils are duly carried into effect in the various establishments ;

(3) The prevention of friction and misunderstanding.

CONSTITUTION

SHOP COMMITTEES

2. There shall be committees for particular shops [1] or groups of shops in a yard,[2] according to local circumstances.

3. *Employees' Side.*—The number of representatives will vary with the size and complexity of the particular shop, but there shall be at least one representative or steward to each Trade Union having members employed in the shop, unless the number of its members is very small, in which case special arrangements may be made for indirect representation through some other Trade Union representative, or in such other way as may be determined by the Yard Committee.

4. *Appointment.*—The method of appointment of the shop representatives or stewards will be a matter for decision by each Trade Union concerned.

5. *Management Side.*—The official in charge of the shop and his immediate responsible subordinate officials shall form a constant nucleus of the management side.

6. *Number of two sides unequal.*—The numbers on each side of the Committee need not be equal.

DEPARTMENT COMMITTEES

7. There shall be Department Committees in cases where the yard is organized into departments composed of several shops, except in any case in which the need is sufficiently met by the Yard Committee.

8. *Employees' Side.*—The representatives of each Trade Union shall be appointed as may be determined from among their members employed in the department concerned. It is essential that each Union having members employed in the department shall be directly or indirectly represented upon the Department Committee. It is also desirable that the Trade Unions shall arrange the appointment

---

[1] The word ' shop' throughout shall be understood to include any workshop, storehouse or ship, or group of workmen not usually attached to any workshop, storehouse or ship.

[2] The word ' yard ' throughout shall be understood to include any dockyard store depot, or any other Admiralty industrial establishment.

of their representatives in such a way that each shop is represented, as far as practicable, upon the Department Committee.

9. *Management Side.*—The official in charge of the department and his immediate responsible subordinate officials shall form a constant nucleus of the management side.

YARD COMMITTEES

10. There shall be one Yard Committee for each yard.

11. *Employees' Side.*—The appointment of representatives of the employees' side of the Yard Committee shall be made in a manner similar to that for the Department Committee. That is to say, the Trade Unions having representatives upon all the Department Committees shall also be directly or indirectly represented upon the Yard Committee. Further, the principle should also be observed that every department shall be represented upon the Yard Committee.

12. *Management Side.*—The management side shall consist of the Superintendent or other officer-in-charge of the yard, together with such other responsible officers as may be determined. Where such an officer exists the Labour Officer or Welfare Superintendent shall be a member of the Committee.

13. The Yard Committee shall determine what Department or Shop Committees are required to suit the circumstances of each case, and shall also determine any difference which may arise on, or regarding, Department Committees and Shop Committees.

OFFICERS OF THE ABOVE COMMITTEES, PROCEDURE, ETC.

14. *Chairman, &c.*—The Chairman of a Committee shall be appointed from the management side and the Vice-Chairman from the employees' side. Each side shall appoint a Secretary. The Vice-Chairman and the employees' Secretary shall be employed in the establishment concerned.

15. *Period of Appointment.*—The representatives shall be appointed for a period of twelve months and shall be eligible for re-election.

16. *Filling of Vacancies.*—In the event of a representative on a Committee ceasing to be employed in the establishment or being transferred from one shop or department to another, a successor shall be appointed in the ordinary way by the official in charge or Trade Union concerned to hold office for the remainder of the current term of the Committee.

17. *Co-option.*—Either side of a Committee shall have the right to co-opt persons having a particular knowledge of a matter under discussion, in a consultative capacity. The addition shall be made only for the period during which the particular question is before the Committee.

18. *District Official of Trade Union.*—It shall be open for any

Trade Union to arrange for the attendance of its district official at any meeting of the Yard Committee while business particularly affecting the said Union is under discussion. Any Trade Union taking advantage of this clause shall notify the Chairman and Secretary of the management side.

19. *Size of Committees.*—It is undesirable that any Committee should be large, and in practice it will probably be found that not more than twelve members a side will be likely to suit most circumstances.

20. *Regular Meetings.*—Ordinary meetings of the Committees shall be held regularly on specified days, usually not more frequently than once a month.

21. *Special Meetings.*—Special meetings of any Committee shall be called at twenty-four hours' notice, on a request on behalf of one side by its Secretary to the Secretary of the other side. The subject of the meeting shall appear on the notice convening it.

22. *Meetings to be in Working Hours.*—Meetings of Committees shall ordinarily be held during working hours, by arrangement with the management. Accommodation for holding these meetings will be provided by the Yard Authorities.

23. *Circulation of Agenda.*—The agenda shall be submitted by the Secretaries to each member of the Committee at least forty-eight hours before the meeting, except in the case of special meetings. Only business appearing on the agenda shall be transacted at a meeting, except by agreement of both sides.

24. *Minutes.*—Each Secretary of a Committee shall keep Minutes.

25. *Decisions by Agreement.*—Decisions shall be arrived at ordinarily by agreement between the two sides, but a vote may be taken upon any matter of general importance at the discretion of the Chairman.

26. *Procedure for Dealing with Grievances, &c.*—When an individual workman desires to call attention to a grievance or any other matter, he shall do it either through the usual official channel, or he shall report it to his Trade Union representative on the Committee concerned. Such official shall endeavour, in the first instance, to obtain a settlement, but, failing this, he shall inform the Secretary of the employees' side of the Shop Committee, who shall then endeavour to arrange a settlement with the official in charge. If no such settlement is reached, the matter will come before the Shop Committee. In the event of the matter not being settled on the Shop Committee, it can be reported to the Department Committee, and failing settlement there, to the Yard Committee.

27. *Reference to Admiralty Industrial Council.*—In the event of any matter not being decided at the Yard Committee, it shall be open to either side to require its reference to the Admiralty Industrial Council.

28.   *Facilities for Employees' Officials.*—The Secretary of the

employees' side of the Yard Committee shall have full facilities to enter any department or shop in the Yard in the course of his duties as Secretary. Similarly, after acquainting the official in charge of his shop, the Secretary of a Shop or Department Committee shall have full facilities to enter the shop in which such Yard Committee Secretary is employed.

29. *Payment for Attendance.*—The employees' representatives shall be paid their earnings lost for time spent at meetings of the Committees.

30. *Separate Meetings of Employees' Side of Committees.*—Facilities shall be provided for such meetings in the Yard, normally outside working hours.

FUNCTIONS

31. The Shop, Department, and Yard Committees shall consider only matters of a general nature, as indicated in the functions outlined below. Matters which are ordinarily regarded as exclusively trade questions, such as wages, &c., shall not be dealt with on those Committees.

32. In indicating the principal functions which will come within the scope of the Committees, no attempt has been made to demarcate as between the powers of the Shop and Department Committees, or between those of the Department and Yard Committees; but, in practice, the Yard Committee will, of necessity, deal with wider aspects of the subjects indicated than either the Shop or Department Committees.

33. It must also be noted, in the case of some of the functions, that it may have been the rule with certain trades to negotiate on such matters apart from other trades. Where this is the practice, local arrangements should be made accordingly.

34. It is a fundamental principle, in addition, that no Yard Committee (or subordinate Committee) shall have power to make agreements which may be inconsistent with the powers or decision of a Departmental or Trade Joint Council.

35. Matters of a general nature to be dealt with (subject to paras. 31 and 32 above) in full Committee :

(*a*) The issue and revision of works rules.

(*b*) The distribution of working hours ; breaks ; time recording, &c.

(*c*) The payment of wages (time, form of pay ticket, &c.) ; explanation of methods of payment.

(*d*) The settlement of grievances other than those of a specific trade character.

(*e*) Holiday arrangements.

(*f*) Questions of physical welfare (provision of meals, drinking water, lavatories and washing accommodation, cloak-rooms, ventilation, heating and sanitation ; accidents, safety appliances, first aid, ambulance, &c.).

(g) Questions of promotion and reversion.

(h) Questions of discipline and conduct as between management and workpeople (malingering, bullying, time-keeping ; publicity in regard to rules ; supervision of notice boards, &c.).

(i) Terms of engagement of workpeople.

(j) The training of apprentices and young persons.

(k) Technical library, lectures on the technical and social aspects of industry.

(l) Suggestions of improvements in method and organization.

(m) Investigation of circumstances tending to reduce efficiency or in any way to interfere with the satisfactory working of the establishments.

(n) Collections (for clubs, charities, &c.).

(o) Entertainments and sports.

APPENDIX H

COLLECTIVE CONTRACT

(See Chapter XV)

The following memorandum, issued under the auspices of the Paisley Trades and Labour Council, was written by two prominent leaders of the workshop movement on the Clyde. Mr. Gallacher has been mentioned in the text as one of the most influential of the ' left wing ' leaders. Since the war he has been active in the Communist movement and is said to have repudiated the views contained in the memorandum. Mr. Paton, who subsequently became Organizing Secretary of the National Guilds League, died in 1920. The memorandum is here reprinted as showing how, on the purely industrial side, the shop stewards' movement was regarded by many of its active members as a means to the securing of ' workers' control ' in the workshop.

TOWARDS INDUSTRIAL DEMOCRACY

A MEMORANDUM ON WORKSHOP CONTROL

By W. Gallacher (Clyde Workers' Committee) and J. Paton (A.S.E.).

Reconstruction.—We would have it clearly understood by all whom it concerns that Labour has nothing to hope for and much to fear from

Industrial Reconstruction, as it is being so freely expounded at present by managing directors, statesmen, and official Trade Union leaders. These gentlemen unite in declaring that there can be no return after the war to the old conditions : there must be ' a complete break with the past'. But the moment they get down to definite proposals it becomes evident that not only do they desire to preserve the very worst evils of the old system, but also to perpetuate as many of the restrictive regulations of war time as the workers can be bribed to submit to. They are weaving snares to our feet in the form of co-partnership and profit-sharing schemes ; their talk is not of freedom, but of security of employment, higher wages, and bonus ; of harmony between employers and wage-earners ; and of that latest abomination, workers' welfare. The central figure of their brightest vision of the future is the profiteer, swollen with the dividends of increased production in the national interest. Behind him stretch his foundries and factories, their furnaces blazing, their machinery clanking by day and by night, manned by an army of sleek, docile, contented wage-slaves. In short, the capitalist system of production having broken down, we are to be invited to build it up again, and re-establish it more securely than ever.

It would appear that we must do our own reconstruction. It is very simple ; there is only one thing to be done, and we can begin to do it now. It is to smash the wage system, and wrest the control of industry from the capitalists. Nothing else is any use at all. No ' break with the past ' is possible under capitalism. Though conditions be ' reformed ' out of all recognition, so long as wagery remains ' the past ' is with us still. The more it changes the more it is the same thing.

Now the movement for the overthrow of capitalism by an abolition of the wages system must begin, not at Westminster, not in the Trade Union Executive, nor yet in the Trade Union branches, but in the workshops. And it should take the form of the assumption by the workers of an ever-increasing share in control.

Not Peace but a Sword.—A share in control does not imply that the workers should enter into partnership or any sort of alliance with the employer, or incur joint responsibility with him, or be identified with him in any way. All forms of co-partnership—collective or individual—are based on the theory that the interests of the exploiter and exploited are identical, whereas they are, in fact, mutually antagonistic and irreconcilable. All such schemes are cunningly designed by a plausible appeal to individual cupidity to corrupt the worker and seduce him from collective action with his fellows. Co-partnership multiplies profiteers and nourishes capitalism. And are we not out to destroy capitalism ?

There must be no alliance or compromise with the employer. We shall be obliged, indeed, to negotiate with him through his representatives in the daily routine of the workshop, but not to espouse his interests, or to advance them in any way when it lies in our power to do otherwise. Our policy is that of invaders of our native province of Industry, now in the hands of an arrogant and tyrannical usurper, and what we win in our advance we control *exclusively and independently*.

The First Step.—The first step should be to establish in every industrial area, and for each industry, a system of Workshop Committees, as follows :

I.—*The Works Committee.*—In every works a Works Committee shall be elected by and from all the Trade Unionists, skilled and unskilled, in the various departments. Each department numbering fifty workers or less shall have one representative on the Committee, and an additional representative shall be granted for every succeeding fifty or part thereof.

II.—*Departmental Committees.*—Each department shall appoint a sub-committee to act in conjunction with, and under the direction of, the Works Committee, and composed of the delegate or delegates to the Works Committee, together with two other Trade Unionists in the department.

III.—*Functions of Departmental Committees :*

(*a*) To see that all Trade Union standards and agreements are strictly observed.

(*b*) To represent the workers in all negotiations with the Departmental Management.

(*c*) To keep a faithful record of all changes in shop customs or practices : a copy of all such records to be supplied to the Works Committee.

(*d*) *To be the sole medium of contract between the firm and the workers*, and to exercise full bargaining powers on behalf of the men and women in the department in fixing time allowance where premium bonus is in operation, and rates where piecework obtains. That is to say, all individual contracting as it is done at present between the workman and the foreman or rate-fixer, is to be eliminated. These negotiations shall in future be conducted only through the Committee.

(*e*) Departmental Committee shall report to the Works Committee weekly.

IV.—*Functions of Works Committee :*

(*a*) To see that all Trade Union standards and agreements are strictly observed throughout the establishment, and to co-ordinate the activities of the Departmental Committees.

(*b*) To represent the workers in all negotiations with the works management.

(*c*) To consult with the works management in all cases where it is proposed to transfer men or women from craft to craft or from one department to another, or in any way to depart from established workshop practice, but to act in these matters only upon representations made by the Departmental Committees.

(*d*) To keep a faithful record of all changes in shop customs and practices. A copy of all such records to be forwarded to and systematically filed by the Allied Trades Committee mentioned in Clause V hereinafter.

(*e*) The Works Committee shall report to the Allied Trades Committee weekly.

V.—*The Allied Trades Committee.*—In each district, and for each industry, an Allied Trades Committee shall be appointed, composed of the district officials of the Trade Unions concerned, skilled and unskilled.

VI.—*Functions of Allied Trades Committee.*—To co-ordinate the methods and activities of the Works Committees, and to act as Court of Appeal in all matters relating to conditions in the workshops in the district, and as sole intermediary between the Workshop Committees and joint bodies of employers—Employers' Federation and the like, State Committees, Government Departments, &c.

Note.—When the workers have expelled the capitalist and taken over complete control of the entire industry, the main function of the Allied Trades or District Committee will be the effective and economical distribution of labour throughout the district, thus rendering superfluous anything in the nature of a State labour exchange. For the present, however, that function should be exercised with caution and restraint, and only where it will be clearly to the advantage of Labour and not merely of the employer. Skilful manipulation of supply and demand of labour might be employed strategically over the area by an alert District Committee as a means of forcing up wages and strengthening the position of the Works Committees in particular firms.

In organizing ' direct action ' the Committees will be invaluable.

Solidarity.—Such a system as we have sketched would promote solidarity amongst the workers by substituting collective for individual bargaining, and amalgamation would be advanced by the simple method of ignoring craft and class prejudices and working together as though it were already an accomplished fact. Amalgamation cannot be brought about in any other way. Trade Union officials will never give an effective lead to a movement the success of which involves obscurity or social ruin for great numbers of themselves. But let the advantages of unity be clearly demonstrated in practice in the workshops, and the Trade Union Executives will soon be compelled by the overwhelming pressure of the rank and file to broaden the basis of organization. We shall have taken a long stride in the direction of Industrial Unionism.

The Next Step.—After all, committees are but machinery and solidarity a preliminary to action.   Let us see, then, what the further policy of the committees will be.

Only the apathy or disloyalty of the workers themselves can prevent the Works Committees having in a very short time the experience and the authority to enable them to undertake in one large contract, or in two or three contracts at most, the entire business of production through-out the establishment.   Granted an alliance with the organized office-workers—a development which is assured so soon as the Shop Committees are worthy of confidence and influential enough to give adequate pro-tection—these contracts might include the work of design and the purchase of raw material, as well as the operations of manufacture and construction.   But to begin with the undertaking will cover only the manual operations.   The contract price, or wages—for it is still wages—will be remitted by the firm to the Works Committee in a lump sum, and distributed to the workers by their own representatives or their officials, and by whatever system or scale of remuneration they may choose to adopt.   If, as is likely, a great Industrial Union has by this time taken the place of the sectional Unions, these financial intromissions may be carried out by its District Executive (which would succeed the Allied Trades Committee) instead of by the Works Committee.   A specially enlightened Union of this sort would no doubt elect to pool the earnings of its members and pay to each a regular salary weekly, monthly, or quarterly, exacting, of course, from the recipient a fixed minimum record of work for the period.

An important feature of all contracts would be a clause limiting the responsibility of the committees to the actual business of production. That is to say, they would not be penalized for any stoppage of work from whatever cause, or held liable for losses arising therefrom.   Nor would they accept responsibility for the smooth running of the works, or for tranquillity or efficiency in the industry as a whole.

The Costs of Control.—If it is contended that the scheme here out-lined would make extensive inroads upon the time spent by members of committee at their ordinary occupations, and correspondingly heavy demands upon their fellow-workers who would have to make good their wages, the reply is that the time is spent in the interests of the workers throughout the industry, and the loss in wages should therefore be a direct charge upon Trade Union funds.   And, further, that, wisely directed and adequately supported, the committees will soon see to it that these charges are much more than made good to the workers in the form of increased wages or contract prices.

The point we have to grasp, however, is that we—the workers—*already pay the expenses of management in industry*, although we do not enjoy the privileges.   For whence, if not out of the workers' earnings, come the wages of the army of managers, foremen, bullies, speeders-up, and spies who throng our modern industries ? The number of these functionaries will be greatly reduced in a democratized workshop, and many of the species will be entirely eliminated. The employer on his side, having no longer any interest in control, will pay only a staff of inspectors to ensure that the quality of the workmanship and material he is being supplied with is in keeping with the terms of the contract. The functions of management will have passed to the committees, and it will be their business to see that contract prices amply cover all the costs of these functions. The conveners of the Works Committee and the Departmental Committee will gradually but surely drive out and supplant the works manager and departmental foreman. These conveners then become full-time officials, and will, of course, be elected periodically like the rest of the committees by their fellow-workers.

The Knock-out Blow.—Now it is true that even when we have got so far we shall not yet have destroyed the wage system. But we shall have undermined it. Capitalism will still flourish, but for the first time in its sordid history it will be in real jeopardy. With such a grip on the industrial machine as we have postulated, and backed by the resources of a great Industrial Union, or it might even be a Federation of Industrial Unions, the committees should soon force up contract prices to a point that would approximate to the full exchange value of the product, and put the profiteer out of business. In short, we shall have taken to our hands a powerful economic lever which, intelligently and resolutely applied, is easily capable of overthrowing the entire structure of capitalism, and substituting for it a real Industrial Democracy.

APPENDIX J

COLLECTIVE CONTRACT

(See Chapter XV)

These memoranda were drawn up by a group of shop stewards employed in the Whitehead Torpedo Works at Weymouth. They arose quite independently of the proposals contained in the previous appendix, neither group knowing, until later, what the other was contemplating. They thus illustrate the spontaneous local growth of ideas characteristic of the workshop movement, although, in this case, both sets of proposals obviously owe a good deal to the teachings of the Guild Socialists.

COLLECTIVE CONTRACT
WORKSHOP CONTROL FOR WHITEHEADS'

The invitation offered by the management of the Whitehead Torpedo Works (Weymouth), Limited, to the employees, to co-operate with their representatives in forming a Works Council, compels an immediate discussion of the very interesting subject of workshop control.

As the firm made clear, their suggested scheme is an anticipation of the Works Councils already advocated by a sub-committee of the Reconstruction Committee. The particular province of this sub-committee is the relations between employers and employed, and their findings are outlined in the Interim Report on Joint Standing Industrial Councils, briefly known as the Whitley Report.

We agree with a recent contributor to the *Herald*, that it is difficult to see what is hoped to be accomplished by setting up these Councils, which are certainly a very unambitious project. Nor does the agenda submitted by the firm in their memorandum enlighten us, although it is not our intention to add to the very intelligent and exhaustive criticism already levelled against it.

Our task is to prepare Labour for the coming changes, not, we hasten to observe, with the object of participating on Joint Councils, but to arrange that such changes shall be in fullest accord with the aspirations of organized Labour, and in no way to lessen its power of aggressive industrial action.

We are convinced that, after the war, industry will differ radically from its past, and that it is not possible, even where it is desirable, to return to pre-war conditions. Our safeguard against the triumph of those adversaries whose avarice has been sharpened by the vista of what can be accomplished by industry unfettered by Trade Union restrictions, is to start right now to force the trend of change into the direction we most desire it to go.

There have always been those who have urged a truce in the conflict between Capital and Labour, but never were their voices so loud or so insistent as at the present moment. Writers of all shades of opinion have assembled under the banner of Industrial Peace, and have given us such well written considerations as are found in the Garton Memorandum.

If we examine the findings of these writers and committees, or the remarkable speech of Mr. Neville Chamberlain, at the Trade Union Congress, in September 1916, or again the declarations of many large employers of labour, we discover they are unanimous in their conclusions that the ultimate and unfailing sedative for Labour is that it be given a share in the control of industry. Where they differ is in the degree of control they are prepared to concede to Labour, and in the case of the proposed Joint Standing Industrial Councils there is no suggestion of industrial control, and the extent to which workshop control will be granted is carefully left undefined.

Why do the offerings to Labour assume this unusual form ? We think the answer is to be found in the realization by the more thoughtful employers that intelligent workmen are beginning to revolt against the wage system, with its immoral conception of labour as a commodity ; that the propaganda of the ' Intellectuals ' is turning the gaze of organized Labour towards ' Citizenship and Status '. Upon no other assumption can we explain such significant paragraphs as the following :

> The attitude of a certain section of employers who look on their employees as ' hands ', as cogwheels in the industrial machine, having a market value but no recognized rights as human beings, is bitterly resented. Still more offensive is the attitude which regards the working man as a very good fellow so long as he is kept in his place and requiring to be guided and disciplined, but not to be consulted in matters vitally affecting his interests. Labour has come to know its power. It realizes that it is an indispensable party to the production of wealth, and it requires to be treated frankly as a partner with equal rights and equal responsibilities.— Garton Memorandum.

Or the following from the Whitley report :

> We have thought it well to refrain from making suggestions of offering opinions with regard to such matters as profit-sharing, co-partnership, or particular systems of wages, &c. It would be impracticable for us to make any useful general recommendation on such matters, having regard to the varying conditions in different trades. We are convinced, moreover, that a permanent improvement in the relations between employers and employed must be founded upon something other than a cash basis. What is wanted is that the workpeople should have a greater opportunity of participating in the discussion about and adjustment of those parts of industry by which they are most affected.

From the foregoing quotations we can deduce that not only do our employers and their advisers fully understand the tendency of thoughtful Labour, but they are also prepared to interpret the spirit behind the tendency (for consumption by the general public) as being in complete accord with modern industrialism, and with characteristic effrontery are preparing to take charge of its development. This is the danger which confronts us, and which our modest scheme is framed to avoid. With these observations upon the general situation we will proceed to give the broad outlines of a simple and tentative scheme for workshop control by the employees of Messrs. Whitehead's Torpedo Works.

1. The necessary preliminary would be the election of the Works Committee, fully representative of the different Trade Unions.

2. Individual piece-work would be abolished, and the Committee would undertake work by collective contract.

3. Workmen would be engaged by the Committee, and the hours of work regulated by them. In a like manner, apprentices and their vocational training would be under the entire supervision of the Committee.

There is nothing in these proposals (details of which will be published later) of a revolutionary nature, and it is claimed to be but a short step along the road to Industrial Democracy. The iniquitous wage system would remain, together with control of capital and industry by the capitalist. All that we claim, is that it provides the *only basis* on which the workers can assume any responsibility for workshop management. Unpretentious though it is, we yet aver that it is the most that can be accomplished by Labour whilst its front is weakened by the existence of a multiplicity of sectional organizations. That we may not be misunderstood, we here assert, with all the emphasis at our command, that the most immediate concern of Labour is the perfecting of its organization by the amalgamation of existing societies to the ultimate formation of Industrial Unions.

We are confident that the adoption of our proposals will assist in that direction, by virtue of creating a common interest and removing many local undesirable influences. That it would make for increased comfort whilst in employment there can be no doubt, and it would finally remove the vexatious irritation caused by the intrusion of disciples of the scientific management fraternity, who by the way, are quite old acquaintances masquerading under a new name.

Without dogmatically asserting any economic law, we claim abundant proof that an all-round advance of wages does not bring the increased spending power and consequent comfort expected from it. The advantage is only felt when the advance is restricted to a limited number of workmen, and it could also be demonstrated that the advantage to them is a disadvantage to their fellows. Never, we feel sure, were wage advances of so little concern to Labour. The vicious circle from increased wages to increased prices, or vice versa, whichever it may be, has become as clear as daylight, until it leaves Labour without ambition to achieve anything in this direction except to maintain an accustomed standard of life.

We can assume therefore, as we believe, that wage advances will rapidly become a secondary object of organized Labour, which, if it is not to become stagnant, must of necessity focus its activities in other directions to achieve that progress and industrial amelioration which is its present purpose. Hours of labour, workshop conditions and, to an ever-growing section, the eventual control of industry in partnership with the State, reveal great possibilities of what can be accomplished. What more essential first step can there then be, than that we should assume control of production in the workshop, and, incidentally, the conditions under which we work ? It would prove our capability in a limited degree, while it would also improve our status. Our responsibility would be enhanced, and the ' team spirit ' would be introduced ; both factors from which much is expected.

Be it understood that this is a local development which can be achieved *now*. The discontent of the workmen and the change of front by the management make the moment propitious for a change.

Should our recommendations prove abortive, or be disregarded, we would appeal to the workers to refuse to participate on Joint Councils otherwise than as a separate negotiating body, safeguarding the interests of Labour. This would be no appreciable departure from past procedure, and would remove the danger of Labour compromising in a struggle where compromise means disaster. This point is emphasized by the resolutions of the Employers' Parliamentary Council demanding that agreements drawn up by Joint Councils shall be made legally obligatory upon Trade Unions, and calling for the repeal of the Trades Disputes Act.

The following passage from Mr. G. D. H. Cole's latest and most instructive book [1] explains the position with the characteristic clarity and conciseness of that indefatigable champion of Labour's cause :

> The development of Trade Unionism towards the Guilds must therefore take the form, not of acceptance of joint *responsibility* for the conduct of industry by the Trade Unions, but of increasing *interference* by them in the conduct of industry. Where a whole province of industrial management can be taken bodily out of the hands of the employers and transferred to the workers, well and good ; that is a stage in the evolution of National Guilds ; but until such complete transference can take place in any sphere the action of Trade Unions must remain external and, to that extent, irresponsible, if they are to maintain their independence and their freedom to go further.

WEYMOUTH JOINT COMMITTEE OF ALLIED ENGINEERING
TRADES

FELLOW MEMBERS,

You are requested to give your earnest consideration to the subject of the following report, and to attend an aggregate meeting of all piece-workers to be held in the Royal Palm Court, on Sunday, the 13th of October 1918, at 3 p.m., at which a vote will be taken to decide our future policy.

THE JOINT COMMITTEE.

[1] *Self Government in Industry.*

JOINT COMMITTEE REPORT ON AN ENQUIRY INTO THE PRESENT
WORKING OF THE PIECE-WORK SYSTEM

The method of payment to the workers by the system of ' piece-work ' is so well known and understood as to need little definition. Piece-work is one of the most common methods of payment in the engineering trade. To an increasing extent it has superseded the more ancient system of ' day work '.

In spite of Trade Union rules, piece-work is quite often regarded as being more palatable to the workers than day work. Nevertheless, day work had many advantages, which are fast going out of existence under the piece-work system.

The day rate, which has been established as a result of collective bargaining, is a sacred minimum, below which no worker, no matter how slow, shall be paid. It has been established by collective action, increases are sought by collective action, and a reduction would be resisted by collective action. The outstanding characteristic of the day rate is this feature of its being a collective concern of all workers. To the employer it necessitates that discipline and hustle must be enforced by all available means, in order to ensure the maximum output for the minimum payment.

Piece-work has been instituted to secure this end by less costly and more efficient means. It provides the worker with a certain limited, individual, interest in output, by making his earnings depend, to some extent, on the amount of work turned out.

The old collective spirit, which characterized the day-work system, has broken down under the modern development of the piece-work system. In its place there has grown up individual interest, individual anomaly, individual discontent, and the gradual break up of that spirit of harmony and good fellowship that was the pride of the Trade Union movement, when more even conditions obtained, either under the day rate or piece-work with restriction on output. The development of this undesirable tendency necessitates that we should make a survey of the circumstances, if we are to revert again from individual to collective interest in the question of wages and earnings.

It will be found that piece-work prices start off with being uneven. This is due to several causes. The greatest factor in the first making of a price is the individual. Because some individuals are faster than others ; because, also, some have more cheek than others, some are more truthful than others, and for many other reasons and circumstances, prices are made uneven to start with. This can be overcome by authorizing gang committees to concern themselves more with all new prices. By thus making the problem of price making less an individual and more a collective concern, prices would be made which would better conform to some even standard. Even though such methods may tend to make prices more even, some unevenness is bound to persist. The unevenness complained of does not, however, start and finish with price making.

A price made for a job when only small numbers are turned out increases in value to the worker when the same job is turned out in larger quantities. Hence, any unevenness in the first instance becomes magnified under such a circumstance. The advantages from the increased speed, made possible with larger quantities, are greater on some jobs than others; hence a further reason why prices are uneven. Often a man with a bad price on a job will try to get an inflated price on a new job to compensate him; a man with a good price will not be so concerned if his new price is not so inflated; this is a very prolific source of unevenness in prices. The raising of a non-mechanical test, such as air-pressure test, may cause a large proportion of a certain part to be scrapped in an early operation. This may result in a disproportionate rate of production in some operation. The effect may be an increase of production in the most profitable, or else the least profitable operation. This also is a cause of unevenness in prices. Then some jobs afford more scope than others for ' scamping ' and ' war finish ' and a minute saved on the machine may cost an hour on the bench. This demoralizing, downward trend towards the ' shoddy ' must be admitted, with feelings of injured pride, to be a most powerful factor in the unevenness of prices. The causes of unevenness are too numerous and ofttimes too difficult to explain away. Nevertheless the plain fact remains that unevenness is inevitable, and is admitted. That it has always been recognized as undesirable and harmful is shown by the fact that many rough and ready methods have been adopted by the workers to overcome and nullify the tendency.

In the past, a worker on a bad paying job would get his turn on a good paying job; or else the other expedient of ' giving hours ' by one of the more favoured to one of the less fortunate. These rough and ready practices obtained mostly when the collective spirit existed, and have gone out of use with the advent of the individual spirit, resulting from speeding up. There can be no collective action while unevenness exists. Only discord and disunity can result from the individual division that has sprung up in the question of piece-work earnings.

To overcome the evil, it has been suggested that a half-way house might be found in the re-adjustment of some prices at each end of the scale. A ballot taken on this proposal resulted in a majority of two to one in favour. The Joint Committee, in accepting this as a mandate to act, are anxious to take the wisest and most expedient course ; believing that it is better to take time and act wisely than to act rashly in a hurry.   They believe that to adjust the extreme high and low prices will palliate the evil, but will not cure it ; rather will it leave the cancer to work further ravages till a fresh occasion may demand a fresh use of the surgeon's knife.

There is only one complete cure ; that is collective or fellowship piece-work over a large area ; over the whole factory for preference. The Joint Committee being aware that this principle exists in many parts of the country, and that it is a principle that is being adopted to an increasing extent as a means of curing this same evil, set up a sub-committee to enquire into the principle and report on same.

This Committee is able to report that collective piece-work offers many advantages over individual piece-work.   It is much more simple and more efficient.   It restores the old collective spirit securing collective effort, collective interest, and harmony.   No drastic changes would be required.   For instance :

The individual prices could still remain on the cards as at present. The whole of the workers who took part in collective piece-work would be required to put in their best efforts.   They would be paid out their day-rate earnings off the time clocks, as at present.   The whole of the day-rate earnings of the men who took part on collective piece-work would be totalled up.   For the sake of example we will suppose the total to be £500.   The value of all cards relating to finished work for the corresponding period would also be totalled up, and amounted to, say £1,000.   It can be seen that there is now a total balance of £500 to be paid amongst all those who have taken part in the work. It must be shared out according to the time each man has worked, also according to the various day rates of those engaged.   To do this is very simple, for in the example we have given the total balance is 100 per cent. of the total day-rate wages.   Therefore, as each individual day-rate wage is known, we have simply to pay out an individual balance of 100 per cent. of each amount.

In so far as the two methods, individual and collective piece-work, are compared with each other, it is in this matter of calculation and book-keeping that all the advantage is shown to be with the collective method.   For, with several thousand individual piece-work jobs, there must of necessity be several thousand intricate calculations. Whereas with the collective method, no matter how many thousands of separate jobs there may be, they are all totalled up, and one calculation only will define the amount of piece-work balance to be paid to each individual.   The relation of total piece-work earnings to total day-work earnings is declared to result in a balance of so much per cent.   Payment can then be made of the balance at just that ' so much per cent.' of each man's individual day-rate earnings.   When this method is once understood it should commend itself to the majority of workers.

No one would urge that a fellow worker, whose speed is greater or less than his own, should take a higher or lower percentage of piece-work balance; but some will urge that it would be unfair for the man who slacks to take the same percentage as the others. It would be open to any one to bring a charge of slacking against another, and proper means should be afforded for making and defending such a charge. It is expected that the existence of such machinery for dealing with slacking would provide a complete cure for such an evil.

It is clear that if slacking tended to become at all general, its effect would be shown in a decrease of percentage of piece-work balance. This in itself would cause a search to be made for the cause, and would find its own remedy. But while general slacking would provide its own cure, some individual slacking might conceivably persist in spite of all ordinary methods to eliminate it. We suggest one definite remedy for the hard case. Means must exist for isolating an aggravated case of slacking. If any one slacks to such a persistent extent as to constitute a grievance on the part of the general body, such a person must be set to work on individual piece-work, on jobs which are known to be priced at the average rate of earnings, or less.

But slacking is not expected from the collective method of working piece-work; rather the reverse. It is expected to set up harmony in the place of discord; evenness of earnings in the place of inequality; the collective spirit in the place of individual division. The argument about the possible unfairness of a possible slacker is ill-founded, for it cannot be compared with the existing unfairness of unequal individual piece-work prices. Incidentally, it should be observed that the sliding scale of prices for apprentice rates would cease to exist with the collective principle, thereby removing the chief inducement to the abuse of apprentice labour. We see then that on all counts collective piece-work would cure evils, not create them.

It is inevitable with such a proposal that the argument about slacking will be advanced, and although it is easily answered, to answer it is not enough. For the argument will not be advanced by those who wish to help the change to come about, but by those who, with quite honest intentions, resent any change. The first introduction of individual piece-work was resented by those very same people for the very same reason. Strangely enough the institution whose advent they once opposed they will now wish to conserve. After all of their arguments have been met and answered they will, for the lack of argument, claim that this proposal would mean ' moving too fast '. This is an odd accusation to level against the Trade Union movement; yet it is perhaps well that we should draw attention to the dangers of going too slow.

No one will deny that the process of speeding up has caused a search-light to be focussed upon the question of piece-work prices. The Joint Committee has all too much evidence to know that many of the higher prices are, and have been, subjects of attack. And while the practice of re-designing, and therefore re-pricing, certain jobs have been confined to a few, it is the straw which shows which way the wind blows. Added to this kind of evidence, which is in the possession of the Joint Committee, it has been openly hinted, and openly declared, ' that there are some prices which *they* will not dream of paying as soon as they get an opportunity of paying less.'

It is unfortunate, even if it is natural, that this price cutting, affecting as it does one job here and one job there, often passes without being noticed by more than the few who are closely affected. That is the evil of individual piece-work. This evil would not exist with collective piece-work, because any attempt at cutting prices would concern us collectively and would invoke collective hostility. Collective piece-work would banish the possibility of being hit in the weakest spot.

To resent change is natural, more natural for some than for others ; but change will not be prevented by marking time. To mark time is to ignore the dangers of drifting backward. Whosoever invites it, and whosoever resents it, *change has got to be.* Signs are too numerous to show that these times are pregnant with many changes.

We dare not ignore the ominous significance in the frequent use of the word ' Reconstruction ' by the enemies of Labour. Reconstruction, as they mean it, gives us nothing to hope for and much to fear. Our opponents are united in declaring that ' there can be no return after the war to the old conditions ' ; there must be ' a complete break with the past '. If we would prevent them from weaving snares for our feet we must do our own reconstruction.

There is only one attitude for the Trade Unions to take : they must not fear changes ; they must subscribe to them. It is our obligation to observe the signs, to face the facts, study figures, reason out conclusions, and from these to point out the wise and the safe path.

INDEX